Rising Above the Influence

A True Story About Alcohol, Drugs and Recovery

Rising Above the Influence

A True Story About Alcohol, Drugs and Recovery

Stephen J. Della Valle

Oak Ridge Press

Rising Above the Influence:
A True Sotry About Alcohol, Drugs, and Recovery
Copyright © 2008 Stephen J. Della Valle
Published by Oak Ridge Press

For further information, please contact:
jasoncraig@att.net

Book design by:
Arbor Books, Inc.
19 Spear Road, Suite 301
Ramsey, NJ 07446
www.arborbooks.com

Printed in the United States of America

Rising Above the Influence:
A True Sotry About Alcohol, Drugs, and Recovery
Stephen J. Della Valle
1. Title 2. Author 3. Addiction & Recovery

Library of Congress Control Number: 2007941832

ISBN 10: 0-9801776-0-X
ISBN 13: 978-0-9801776-0-2

To my wife, Donna—without her,
I wouldn't be where I am today.

Acknowledgments

Thanks to Elise Vaz at Arbor Books for listening to every word I said for the last year and a half. Thanks also to Jessica Gorham and Chris Chella, also at Arbor Books, for their assistance in making this book come to life.

Prologue

There is nothing worse than being locked up, but by the age of thirty-two, I'd pretty much gotten used to it. Theft, drug possession, under the influence, assault—I was arrested all the time, put away for the same things over and over again. For me, it wasn't just a losing streak; it was a way of life.

So when I woke up one night—or maybe it was morning, I sure didn't know—in a cell at Newark's Green Street jail, I wasn't too surprised to see the concrete walls surrounding me, the bars locking me in. I took a deep breath and smelled the familiar odor that only a basement penitentiary could cultivate: moldy, sweaty, rank. Everything was just as it should be. I felt like I'd come home from a short vacation.

I sat up in the bunk where I'd passed out, and I held my head in my hands, wondering what I'd done to get locked up again. For the life of me, I couldn't remember, though I guessed that it must've been something pretty bad—my whole body ached, and I was covered with bruises. The cops had probably roughed me up, sure, but this kind of hurt only came from someone who was really angry, someone who wanted me to pay for what I'd done to them.

There were the usual guards outside my cell—I knew them all by name—and for a minute, I considered calling one of them over and asking him just what the hell I was doing there, but then I stopped myself. I was afraid I'd done something terrible; I was hoping that I hadn't killed anyone. This wasn't the first time I had blacked out.

So I just sat. And sat. And waited and waited. Not that I had much of a sense of time anyway—all I did those days was wander the streets, fucked up and looking for money that would help me stay fucked up—but I knew for sure that inside a jail cell, time ceased to exist. Seconds became hours; minutes turned into months.

I guessed that I'd only been there half a day or less, but checked myself for signs of gray hair and a long beard, just in case.

After listening to more than my fill of howling, mumbling and pleading from the cells around mine, I was relieved to see a man in a suit come into the jail. I didn't recognize his face, but I knew his demeanor: This was a public defender, coming to hear my side of the story and decide the quickest way to make me less of a burden on the court system.

I laughed. *My side of the story doesn't exist, pal*, I thought as a guard let him into the cell.

The guy was looking at some papers in a folder, not really paying attention to me and kind of talking to himself. I guessed he was reading up on my illustrious criminal career and my preferred customer status at Green Street. I stayed sitting on the bunk, looking up at him sleepily, wondering how long the meeting would take. I wanted to get back to bed. Nothing else seemed to matter.

Finally, he looked at me—in fact, he did a double take. He sort of grinned, and that immediately pissed me off.

"What the fuck are you smiling at?" I asked him, starting to stand up, my sore legs wobbling underneath me.

The guy held his hands up. "Relax," he said. "I'm not laughing at you."

I hesitated for a minute and then sat back down slowly, keeping my eyes on him the whole time.

"I just—" he went on, looking almost disturbed, and then he stopped and put his hands down at his sides. "You're Stephen Della Valle, aren't you?"

I narrowed my eyes at him. "That's what it says on those papers there, genius," I answered. For a man with a big college degree, he wasn't impressing me.

"Well, yeah, but we went to grade school together, too. I thought the name sounded familiar, but then when I saw you—well, I recognized you."

I stared at his face; it wasn't ringing any bells. "Sorry," I said. "I don't remember you at all."

"That's okay, man," he said, "that's okay. Just...*wow*. I can't believe it, it's been so long. What the fuck *happened* to you?"

PART ONE

Chapter 1

I was seven or eight years old and I was walking down the street with my mom in Newark, New Jersey. I could never keep up with her—at five feet tall and 100 pounds, Mom was a quick mover no matter what she was doing, and she generally walked about a half a block ahead of me. She'd look back from time to time, to make sure that I was still with her, but she always just kept going at her own pace. Back then, kids weren't snatched off the streets like they are now, so there was no reason for her to hold on to me at all times, and besides, I kind of enjoyed the independence.

So I was straggling along behind her, as usual, when two older women came toward us on the sidewalk. They lived in our neighborhood, and I kind of recognized them. As they passed Mom, they smiled politely at her. As they passed me a few steps later, one of them whispered to the other, "Do you know she's dying of cancer?"

I looked ahead at my mom, hale and hearty and practically sprinting down the street. Her hair was perfectly styled, her dress was clean and pressed, and she held her head high, with a real sense of purpose. She never looked anything other than perfect to me. At that young age, I only had a vague idea of what cancer was, but I knew that she certainly didn't look like she was dying.

When I was a kid, I lived in the North Ward section of Newark with my parents, Eleanor and Nicholas, and my siblings—Vinny, the oldest, Nicky, who came next in line, and Anne, who was the youngest of all of us. We lived in a house, on the first floor, with my grandparents upstairs. My grandfather had come to America from Italy years earlier, by himself, to work and make enough money to bring his family over. A while later, he sent for his wife and his daughter—my mother, who was just a little girl at the time.

Our neighborhood was pretty much entirely Italian, so from the beginning, I was immersed in that culture. Mom, Dad and Vinny all spoke the language at home, and it was all I heard out in the community as well. I thought this was just the natural way of things; I didn't even know that there were people who *weren't* Italian until I started school.

To support our family, Dad worked for the Continental Can company. He didn't make much; we were poor, but so was everyone else we knew, so I didn't know the difference. Despite that, though, I had a decent early childhood. I went to school and I had friends; I was really close with my cousin Bobby, who lived in the same neighborhood. We slept over each other's houses a lot and basically, life was simple. I did all the normal things that normal kids did.

All that changed, of course, once Mom really did start getting sick. No one ever talked about her cancer, not even her—*especially* not her. She had always been a very proper woman, very private, never complaining about anything. So, to keep things normal, we all just had to just go on like nothing out of the ordinary was happening, even when she started getting chemotherapy treatments and lost all her hair.

Back then, in the 1960s, breast cancer was even more of a death sentence than it is today, and Mom was only in her 30s when she was diagnosed. She really was cut down in the prime of her life, as they say; she started out as a busy, active mother and wife and by the end of it, turned into a bedridden ghost of herself. I was terrified, sad and a lot of the time, confused. After all, I couldn't even talk to anyone about what was going on in my own house.

Because Mom was pretty much laid up during many of my formative years, I think that I never got the guidance I should have as a young kid. Dad tried his best to keep the rest of us together, but all his time was dedicated to taking care of his wife and going to work. Those were the only two things he did. Of course, I don't hold any of that against either of them. They were just doing what they had to in a really difficult situation.

Because of it, though—because Mom and Dad were essentially absent from my everyday life—I never had to take responsibility for my actions. Once I started school, I never did homework, and no one told me that I had to. No one ever asked where I'd been when I was out, and I was never punished for doing something "bad." I was pretty much left to my own devices, to figure things out as I went along.

I also wasn't taught how to do a lot of the really basic tasks that every kid was supposed to learn. No one told me how to brush my teeth properly, how to make my bed or where to wash when I took a bath. These may seem like small, inconsequential things, but when you realize as an adult that you don't know how to do any of them, the impact is a little more profound.

My brother Vinny was a musician in his younger days and when he was seventeen or so, he went out on the road with a band for a while. I recently found some letters that my mother had written to him during that time; she was still feeling pretty good then, before she got really sick.

I realized through reading these letters that Vinny had really gotten the benefit of having a happy, normal family much more than I ever had. He'd had parents—real parents with no problems—and he hadn't been alone all the time. He'd been encouraged to pursue his dreams and disciplined when he'd done something wrong. To me, reading those letters was like looking into the life of a stranger—that's how unrecognizable the people described in them were.

I don't begrudge my brother that happiness, though. He's always been like a father figure to me due to our age difference, and I can't be mad at him for the good times he had with our mother. In a way, I'm just content to know that those times even existed.

When I think back on my own relationship with my mother, mostly I just remember her being sick all the time. I don't recall much affection, but I understand that her illness probably prevented it. As she got worse and worse, my Aunt Louise—Bobby's mother, Mom's sister—gave me the maternal attention that I needed. She hugged me a lot, and she cooked me dinner, and she let me stay at her house, playing with Bobby, for as long as I wanted.

The more time I spent there, though, the more I noticed a real difference between my cousin's life and my own. My aunt and uncle were always at his baseball games, cheering him on; they ate dinner together every night. It was such a loving home, and they really seemed to enjoy their togetherness. That was something I'd never experienced myself, so they were the closest thing to a "normal" family that I knew at the time. I loved them, but I always felt *different* around them.

All of this, though, it's not an excuse. You hear a lot of people with addictions and other problems blaming it all on their bad childhoods, but I am not one of those people. Yes, I had it rough sometimes, but I do believe that everything I've done—all the problems I've caused and all the trouble I've been in—is totally my fault. I never robbed anyone or got high because I didn't get enough hugs as a kid. My parents, I believe, did the best they could with the cards they were dealt.

I was just headed down a dead-end road from the beginning, and there was nothing they, or anyone else, could have done to stop me.

Chapter 2

In 1963, Newark was a combat zone. Physically, it was a wreck: the potholed streets were lined with abandoned warehouses and burnt-out stores, and when those were finally knocked down, there were just empty lots for miles. The place was a madhouse most of the time—crime was high, violence was common, and there was nothing anyone could do to stop it. Many crimes, even murders, went unpunished. It was truly a time of lawlessness in a city that hadn't seen better days in a long time.

Newark's population had shifted from mostly white to mostly black over the previous couple of decades, and while that in and of itself wasn't necessarily a bad thing, most people's adjustment to the change had not gone very smoothly. Basically, most people hated anyone who was not of their own color.

With all this racial tension, and everything else going on in the streets—robberies, drugs, killings—the Newark police really had no hope of controlling their own city. They were a large force but, even so, the task was just too overwhelming.

Cops were mostly white and mostly Italian at the time—if you met that description back then, you either joined the Mafia, became a drug addict or signed up for the police department—and they didn't exactly like anyone who was *not* Italian. In their uniforms, with their big mustaches (which every one of them seemed to have), they all looked exactly the same. If any black citizens were "lucky" enough to be cops then, I sure as hell didn't see them.

I turned twelve that year and started junior high. My elementary school career had been fairly uneventful, so I didn't know what to expect from this new place—I'd heard that it was pretty rough and, to be honest, I went into it a little apprehensively.

The first thing I learned was that there were no cliques, like the ones you see in the movies—there were no jocks, no nerds, no popular crowd and no teachers' pets. The only division that existed was racial. There were whites and there were blacks, and whichever you were, you stayed away from the other. End of story.

My second lesson was that to survive, you really had to do what everyone else was doing. You had to be part of a gang—not necessarily a violent one, like a *gang*, but a big group who looked out for each other. I fell in with some Italian kids like myself who hung out every afternoon on the corner of Summer Ave.

Once in this gang, I realized that everyone around me was doing drugs. And drinking, of course—one rarely existed without the other. Finding myself suddenly surrounded by a bunch of people who did this stuff constantly, and wanting to fit in, what do you think I did?

I started out just drinking—beer, mostly, which I got for free from my friends. I drank with them as a recreational activity and based on that, they liked me; even as the new kid, I'd show up and there'd automatically be a six-pack in my hand.

Believe it or not, at first, I hated drinking. I couldn't stand the taste of the beer and I didn't like that it made me have to urinate every ten minutes. Usually, I'd down one can and then make like I had to go to the bathroom so that I could pour the rest of the six-pack out in secret. I just couldn't keep up with the other guys as far as drinking went, and I didn't want to look like a wimp.

I had a lot of trouble being my own person around that crowd—in fact, I found it almost impossible to say no to anything they suggested. I wanted to be liked, and I wanted to feel safe, and I knew that both of those things would happen if I just played along.

So, when one of the guys told me that he could give me something much better than beer, I took it without question. He handed me a bottle of cough medicine and a couple of sleeping pills, and I downed them both. These two narcotics put together produced a heroin-like high that was truly unlike anything I had ever felt before. It made me feel euphoric and confident, like I could handle anything—like I could fight King Kong and win. I immediately fell in love with it. I felt like I'd finally found my purpose in life.

A whole new world opened up to me when I started doing this stuff, and I could see that everyone in the school was doing it, too—and I mean *everyone*. I didn't know a single kid in junior high who wasn't getting high on a daily basis. And it was all so easy to get, even inside the school—we'd cop in the hallways and the bathrooms, where we congregated to smoke instead of going to classes.

Once, a friend asked me how many days a week I got high, and I answered, "Eight"—like the habit was like a job that I loved, and I was willingly putting in overtime. Before long, it was my goal to stay high all the time.

While all of this was going on, I had another chemical surging through my bloodstream, too: hormones. I was turning into a relatively healthy teenage boy and, not surprisingly, my interest in girls grew by the day. Of course, the ones I liked didn't always like me back, and I didn't always like the girls who took an interest in me. But once in a while, things clicked and I got a date or two.

Unfortunately, though, as with any typical teenage romance, it always ended in heartbreak. I took the breakups really hard—my stomach would be in knots, and I would obsessively think about the girl who'd gotten away. It seemed as though the only way to get over the rejection was to get high, to turn back to the one thing that gave me any kind of solace from the harsh reality I was stuck in: my drugs.

Chapter 3

Junior high was very scary. There were assaults at the school every day and the streets outside were no better; there was always something going on, no matter where I was. Sometimes, I looked around me and wondered, *How can Mom and Dad send Anne and me out into a world like this?*

I often had to protect my little sister from danger, and many times, she had to fend for herself. Because of the situation at home—because my parents were so wrapped up in Mom's illness—no one really noticed that it might not be entirely safe to send us to school some days. Anne and I never had much emotional security because of our disconnected home life, and at the time, it seemed to me that going to school just made everything worse.

I felt stronger, though, when I had something in me—a bottle of Robitussin AC and a couple of pills usually did the trick. Back then, because cough syrup had such potent medicine in it, we couldn't buy it over the counter in New Jersey, but we could get it in New York pharmacies for $1.35 a bottle—the only thing it required was a signature. My friends and I took the number 44 bus into the city all the time to get our supplies.

As for the pills, there was one crooked doctor in Newark who had no problem writing prescriptions for money, and every addict in town knew who he was. This guy's waiting room was always packed with people in need of a fix—his business was really booming. He was also known for his attraction to boys, and given his clientele, he probably had his pick of desperate souls to choose from. Not surprisingly, this doctor was later arrested and put in jail for various offenses against his profession's ethical code.

More and more, I retreated into my group of friends, if only for the feeling of safety in numbers. I was definitely one of the guys around them; I went along with almost everything they did, even when we started stealing cars—I was always the lookout, and enjoyed riding around in the backseat while one of the other guys drove.

I also just went with it when it came to fighting, which we seemed to do a lot. Once, we were hanging out on Summer Ave. as usual, and a group of black kids came up from the nearby projects. They were looking for trouble, so we got into a confrontation, and it quickly turned into an all-out brawl.

While I was fighting, a couple of motorcycle cops rolled up. One of them handed me his nightstick so I could better defend myself against the black guys. The cops were far from alarmed about the situation; they just sat there and watched, looking kind of amused.

In my gang, I was respected for doing crazy shit. People always said that I had no fear, but in reality, I wasn't as tough as they all thought. I just never let my fear show, never let anyone know what was really going on inside me. Maybe that was something I learned at home, during all the years when my mother was sick.

I got arrested for the first time while I was in junior high, but from this far away, after so many other run-ins with the law, I couldn't tell you why. I was probably high at school or on the street, and some officer with nothing better to do dragged me down to the station just for the heck of it.

I *do* remember my dad coming down to the precinct, where they were holding me in a cell. I thought that he would just bail me out but instead, right there in the station, he gave the cop who arrested me $50 to make it all go away—and it *worked*. It might seem alarming in this day and age but back then, police corruption was entirely given. It was not an exception to the rule. The guy just took the money and let me go and none of us—Dad, me *or* the cop—were at all surprised. And that's the way things were in Newark.

Just as I was getting ready to leave junior high and move on to high school, Mom's health took another turn for the worse. She was so sick, lying in bed all the time with a tremendous cough. I could hear her from my room at night; it was an endless sound that became deafening just from the repetition.

Mom was on a lot of different medications then, and she kept the bottles lined up on her nightstand. Sometimes, I'd walk into her room and lean right across her weak body to pick up some of those bottles. I'd pop out a few pills for myself and swallow them right there, as she watched. The pain in her eyes, the disappointment at seeing her young son doing such a horrible thing, her powerlessness to stop me—it all should have made me feel guilty. But it didn't. In fact, on the whole, I just didn't feel much of anything anymore.

Chapter 4

If I took everything I hated about junior high and multiplied it by about a thousand, that would be the perfect picture of Baringer High School, where I went next. From my first day there, I was surrounded by more violence, more drug use and more reasons for me to get high and tune it all out than ever before.

To start with, every student who entered the building was patted down for weapons, but that was kind of a joke because we all still managed to sneak in whatever we wanted. I brought knives and stuff all the time—you just had to know how to hide them where they wouldn't be found. A few times, the teachers patting me down even knew that I was carrying—they actually felt the weapons on my person—and they just let me slide on through. They were white and Italian, I was white and Italian, and that was just how it went, like they were telling me, *It's all right. We know you have to protect yourself from **them**.* It certainly made me wonder what the teachers were packing themselves.

The racial segregation was worse than ever. Black and white students even had to go in separate doors, just to keep us all apart and give us fewer chances to start a brawl. Once we were inside, though, it was all fair game and at the drop of a hat, the entire school could be involved in a riot. Once, I even stood up on a table in the cafeteria and threw a chair into the middle of a group of black kids, just to start some shit, just for fun. I incited the whole place—it exploded like fireworks. Everyone was beating the hell out of each other, and I jumped right in the middle and joined them.

When I first started out in high school, I was still drinking cough medicine and popping pills. The high I got from that stuff was just tremendous; it lasted all day and really made school a lot easier to bear. I still drank alcohol, too, as it was the catalyst—the thing that would lead me to the drugs that I *really* wanted to use.

After a while, one of the guys in my group introduced me to heroin. He seemed reluctant to give it to me, like he was concerned about my well-being. "Are you *sure* you want to try it?" he kept asking me, for some reason unhappy with the "yes" answer I gave him every single time.

When I finally did try the stuff, of course, I liked it, though I wasn't quite ready to give up my syrup and pills for it just yet. I continued using those and occasionally, when a friend had some heroin to give away, I went with that. Just like with anything new I tried, I never went out looking for it myself.

When I was fifteen years old, I got a job at a pizzeria. They gave me a '55 Chevy that I drove around Newark, delivering pizzas to the projects and the local unwed mothers' homes. It didn't matter that I had no driver's license; if the cops stopped me, I just told them who I was delivering for, and they let me go. Like I've said before, there were lots of Italians in Newark, and most of us stuck together.

Anthony, my boss—we all called him Batman, for some reason—was a pretty tough guy, but he took a liking to me, I guess. Once, when I got into a fight at school and was told that I had to bring my dad in to talk to the teacher, I brought Anthony instead. Because of what was going on at home, my dad was not involved in my educational career at all, and I didn't tell him that I'd been suspended. I hadn't even brought home a report card in years.

So, Batman came in to the school wearing his white pizza-making uniform, and he sat there in front of my teacher, listening to her complain about me and kicking me in the leg every so often to reprimand me. It was just about all I could do to not fall off my chair laughing. The teacher must have thought that my "father" was crazy.

Of course, I'm not discounting my dad. He wasn't involved in my day-to-day life because he was taking care of my mom, and as I've already said, I understood all that. I knew that it was just how things had to be. And I knew that while Dad wasn't going to ask me how my day was or take me outside for a game of baseball after school, I also knew that when I really needed him, he would be there. He may not have given me a lot of guidance in life or anything, but he certainly bailed me out of any trouble I got myself into—and I got in trouble pretty often.

Case in point: When I was sixteen, I was walking on the boardwalk with some friends, at the beach in Seaside Heights, New Jersey. Out of the blue, a guy just came up and hit me, so hard that I fell to the ground in a daze. When I stood back up, a friend slipped a knife into my hand; the guy came at me again, and I stabbed him. A few times. Okay, a lot of times.

I handed the knife off to someone in my group, who got rid of it just as every cop in Seaside drove up. I was arrested for assault with a deadly weapon—which they couldn't find, so I was able to say that it wasn't me who'd stabbed the guy. How could they prove it with no weapon? I guess it was a lucky break.

Dad stepped in then and got me a lawyer. He also talked to the other guy's dad—you know, in a man-to-man, *Let's straighten out this crazy thing our sons did* kind of a way. When the court date came, the kid actually said that I was not the person who had attacked him. I didn't know what his motivation was, and I wasn't about to ask.

On top of that, the judge took one look at my nemesis, who was six feet tall, and then took in my five-foot frame, and concluded that if there had been a fight between us, it most likely had not been a fair one. The case, miraculously, was thrown out. I may have gotten probation, but it was certainly a lot less than I deserved.

After that, the kid and I sort of became friends. I guessed that my drastic measures had impressed him—my over-the-top retaliation to his attack had let him know that he shouldn't mess with me again. Where I was from, if someone hit you, you always hit him back, even if you knew you didn't stand a chance of winning the fight. You earned respect that way and I guess that's what happened between us.

Chapter 5

Though I was never arrested for such a serious crime again at that young age, I seemed to always be in trouble with the law back then, always getting picked up for being under the influence or for skipping school. One time, I fell asleep in a class and when I woke up, I was arrested by the guy who had been sitting at the desk next to me the whole year—he was an undercover narcotics agent and I guess it was pretty obvious how high I was.

The detective dragged me down to Newark's North Precinct and I told them that I'd gotten the drugs from a black guy. That was always everyone's excuse back then. The cops probably never believed it, but they never said anything because they really just could not have cared less about such a trivial situation. With everything else going on in the city, they didn't have time to investigate some mystery "black guy" who might have sold some drugs to a white kid.

So, in a case like that, Dad would simply come down to the station with $50, and it would all go away. Whatever scrape I was in, big or small, he always got me out of it. He showed up at the jail and bailed me out, or "arranged" it with the cops to let me go. He went to court dates with me and did everything he could to undo or make up for whatever damage I'd caused. He wasn't excusing my behavior, or encouraging it, though I guess he wasn't doing much to stop it, either. My brother Nicky always told Dad to throw me out of the house, but he would never do it.

At least in that one area of my life, I knew I had someone I could depend on to be there when I needed him. I really couldn't say that about anyone else, and I truly believe that my father is the reason why I am even alive today.

By the time I was seventeen years old, I was a full-blown drug addict and all my friends were, too. I had started seeking out heroin on a daily basis, as the cough medicine and pills were getting harder to acquire. Being high all day was pretty much my goal, and school? Well, that kind of became second (or even lower) priority. When I did show up, I slept through classes. When I didn't feel like going at all, I spent my time hanging out in the projects, getting high and then going up to the roof to smoke cigarettes and nod out.

The problem with wanting to be high all day was, of course, having money to do so. I had my pizzeria job but I didn't make much there, and what I did bring home was always gone pretty fast.

I had a friend, though, named Marco, and when I was with him, I always knew we would get high. He often just went right up to drug dealers and robbed them; some willingly gave him whatever they had, because they were so scared of what he might do to them if they didn't. He would also steal drugs from other people we knew; he was a tough guy and had no trouble doing whatever he wanted, and getting what he wanted any way could.

Once, Marco and I went to New York to buy some cough medicine, at a pharmacy that we knew would sell it to us. When the druggist said that he didn't have any of it in stock, Marco picked the guy up by the collar and dragged him over the counter. Suddenly, miraculously, the guy remembered that he *did* have a couple of bottles of what we wanted lying around. We took them and ran, with Marco warning the guy that we'd come back and get him if he called the police.

These days, Marco is doing life in Trenton State Prison for murder, and though I feel bad for him, I can't say that I'm entirely surprised.

Another time in New York, another equally crazy friend and I were hanging out in the subway, just sitting on the steps, feeling high and watching people come and go. Four black guys came up to us and asked for cigarettes, which we knew was a set up, because that was the first thing someone who wanted to rob you said, to get you off your guard. *Uh oh*, I thought through my heroin daze. *We're in trouble now.*

But then, my friend just stood up and shouted, "Get the fuck out of here, you black motherfuckers!" I don't know if it was the cursing, or the yelling, or just the insane look in my friend's eyes, but those guys left us alone. They scampered right off and I felt relieved. They really could have started some shit with us.

Things didn't always have such a happy ending, though. As time went on, and as I sank deeper into the world of addiction, I watched some of my friends slip further away from me, into their own black holes. During that time, a lot of people I knew died. One was a girl I was very close with; we were all just sitting around, getting high, waiting our turns to stick the needle in our arms, and she passed right out. We called an ambulance and it took her away, but we found out the next morning that she hadn't made it. Another close friend of mine was found dead of an overdose behind the wheel of his parked car. He was only nineteen years old.

Because I was so heavily into it by then, I witnessed these events like they were a movie playing on a screen. They were my friends—or at least, they were the people I got high with—but when they died, I really didn't feel anything at all.

Chapter 6

While still caring for my very sick mother, Dad lost his job—another blow to our already fragile family structure. He was laid off because Continental Can, where he'd worked for twenty-five years, decided to move to Michigan. Dad entertained the idea of relocating our family out there, but my mother didn't want to go—she didn't want to leave her own mother behind.

So, we stayed in Newark. Sometimes, I wonder how things would have turned out if only we'd moved to Michigan.

Even though I had never done one page of homework, though I rarely attended classes and slept through most of those that I did show up to, and even though I spent more time at the local police station than I did at my alma mater, I graduated from high school on time, with no problems, at seventeen years of age. I'm not sure how I did it, but I have a feeling that my teachers all just passed me to get me the hell out of there—like they did with pretty much every other kid in the school at the time as well. With everything going on in the city around us, no one was concerned about grades. No one cared if us kids were actually learning anything. All that mattered was keeping things going from day to day, while keeping the violence among students as minimal as possible.

Without school looming over my head anymore—not that I had ever felt any obligation toward the place, but it *had* given me something to do with my time during the week—I was pretty much set adrift on the streets of Newark. I had no plans, no goals, no appointments, no money. My friends and I would get high and hang out at the Treat Theater in downtown Newark, a disgusting establishment that specialized in nonstop porno movies. We didn't go there for that, though—we just liked the theater because no one would bother us there. We could hang out, smoke cigarettes and nod all afternoon, while around us, creepy men came and went, enjoying the entertainment.

Some days, when we had to go into New York to buy cough medicine, we'd go to one of the TV networks—usually CBS—and sit in on the filming of a game show. It was something to do, a warm place to rest and take a nap and enjoy our high.

After graduation, I devoted my life to stealing and getting high—just as I'd done while I was in school, except now, it was a full-time job. My friends and I did a lot of breaking and entering—stores mostly, with apartments or houses here and there—and then sold whatever we'd stolen. There was a certain store in Belleville, run by a guy who would buy just about anything we brought him. Everyone knew this guy, and there was always a parade of characters going in and out of his store—everyone from amateur thieves like myself to big-time truck hijackers who would sell him goods by the case.

One time, in the middle of the night, I got the bright idea to rob a luncheonette. I went down there with a friend named Freddy who was supposed to be my driver and lookout. He drove me to the place and when I couldn't get into the luncheonette through a window or door, I got up on the roof of the building to try to find a way inside. I was hoping to find some sort of access door that I could jimmy open, but the only structure up there was a chimney. Without pondering it a whole lot, I shrugged my shoulders and jumped in.

There were screws sticking out of the bricks inside that chimney, and their sharp ends dug into my body as I slowly inched my way down. After a few excruciating minutes, I finally just let go and fell straight down and out, right onto the luncheonette's grill. Thankfully, the place had been closed for a while by then, and I didn't get my ass burned.

I rolled right over onto the floor, landing hard on my side, then got up on my feet, brushed myself off and went to the front window to make sure Freddy was still outside. He was—his car was parked right out front, running and ready to go—but he was nodded out at the wheel. I yelled and waved my arms, trying to get his attention, but nothing woke him up.

So, I went about my business and tried to find stuff to steal. I pocketed as many packs of cigarettes as I could, and broke into the store's pinball machine for the change. Realizing that there was no real big loot to be scored there without a lot of hassle, I decided to just get out while I was ahead.

Since I couldn't go back out the way I'd come in, my retreat plan involved breaking a window, jumping out and running to the getaway car. I'll admit that I hadn't thought the idea out very well, because if I'd stopped to consider it at all, I probably would have remembered that just about every store window in the city was bulletproof, and encased in iron bars—precautions, I'm sure, that had been installed because of guys like me.

At any rate, despite several attempts to shatter every window in the luncheonette with just about any heavy object I could pick up and hurl, I couldn't get out the way I'd planned. Time was ticking, and I had to be out of the store before daybreak, when someone would come to open things up. Getting caught by a store owner was usually worse than getting nabbed by the police—those guys were really merciless in defense of their own property.

I'd gotten caught by an owner once, and it hadn't been pretty at all. That time, I'd smashed the glass door on the front of a shop to get inside, then gone in with a few plastic bags and started packing stuff into them—cigarettes, money, whatever I could find.

In the middle of my scavenger hunt, the owner had showed up. He was a huge guy, and just the sight of him had stopped me in my tracks. I'd been so scared, I couldn't even run. *Oh shit*, I'd thought, or maybe I'd said it out loud.

Before I'd known what was happening, the store owner had put his huge hand over my face, grabbing my head like a bowling ball. He'd roughed me up good while I'd struggled to get out of his grasp. I'd finally broken loose after what had seemed like hours in his grip, and I'd bolted out the door and down Bloomfield Avenue, a really busy street in Newark.

As I'd run in one direction, a cop going the other way had spotted me and whipped his vehicle around to follow me. He couldn't have known just then what exactly I'd done, but when a guy like me was hauling ass like that, it was a safe bet, for a cop or anyone else, that he was up to no good.

I'd kept running until I'd reached Branch Brook Park, where I was met by a tall, chain-link fence with barbed wire at the top. I'd glanced behind me at the approaching police cruiser, then looked up at the fence and took in a deep breath. There'd only been one way to go from there.

I'd scaled the fence, taking off my shirt at the top and laying it over the sharp bits before throwing myself over and falling right down to the ground, at least ten feet below. Not skipping a beat, I'd jumped right up and kept running, the cops still on my tail.

I'd finally found a hiding spot, and I stayed in there for two hours. At that point, it had grown quiet outside, so I'd figured that the police had moved on to something more serious—surely there had to be something in the city more deserving of their attention than I was.

When I'd climbed back out into the daylight, though, I'd realized how very wrong I had been. Apparently, I'd been public enemy number one that day: The cops had been right there, just waiting for me to come out. When a couple of uniforms had come over to handcuff me, I hadn't put up much of a fight. I'd been tired, dirty and bleeding where the store owner had scratched up my face, and I'd simply hung my head in silence as they'd shoved me in the back of a car and shuttled me down to the Green Street station.

Chapter 7

Back at the luncheonette, I was determined to not get into that kind of situation again. I didn't know who the owner there was, but I still had scars on my face from the last guy, and I didn't want to repeat that scenario at all. Not finding any way out of the store from the front, I ventured into the building's basement, where I found a small window sealed up with putty. I scraped the stuff out with my fingers, and the entire window fell out, frame and all, and I was able to squeeze myself out. Once on the street again, I ran to my waiting getaway car and woke Freddy up. We got out of there fast, before anyone had the chance to call the cops on us.

Breaking and entering, as you can see, wasn't always easy. Sometimes, my friends and I just didn't feel ambitious enough for such an undertaking, so we came up with other means of getting the cash we needed. One of the easiest involved going down to the local cemetery, finding a funeral in progress, and creeping along the line of cars parked near the gravesite, taking purses and whatever else might be of value.

I stole things and sold them almost every day, which meant that I got arrested a lot—not because I was a bad criminal, but simply because the frequency of my crimes upped the chances of my getting caught. I got to know the Newark police force really well during that time. It was still an era of extreme lawlessness in the city, however, so even though the cops dragged me down to the precinct as often as they could, I was rarely held for long. They just couldn't be bothered with a petty thief most of the time, and as soon as my dad could get there with their payoff money, they'd turn me loose, back into the city to do it all over again.

When things got too hot for me—when the cops were picking me up too often, and I was just feeling too much pressure in my everyday life—I got the idea to go into rehab, to escape for a while. In those few years after high school, I did it a couple of times, not because I wanted to stop using drugs but just to get some time away from everything. It was like a vacation for me, not a real attempt to get clean. I never, ever had any intention of quitting my bad habits.

Rehab in the late '60s was much different than it is today. It wasn't some touchy-feely, spa-like retreat where you sat in a circle and talked about your feelings all day, and everyone hugged you and cried. Back then, they'd cut your hair and make you wear a diaper, belittle you whenever they could, and do anything possible to break your self-esteem down to nothing. For most people who ended up in rehab, who had little self-esteem to begin with, this was a horrifying and humiliating experience. As a cure for addiction, it didn't work for anyone I knew.

The first time I checked myself into a rehab center, I was pretty shocked at what was going on. I hadn't thought it would be a party, but the inhumane environment I was put into was just beyond my comprehension. The place was run like a military boot camp; no lie, they even made me scrub a bathroom with a toothbrush. It was so incredibly obvious that this was the absolute wrong approach, but the "counselors"—largely ex-addicts themselves—seemed to really get off on the abuse, which they doled out freely.

Because I didn't care much about being there in the first place, and because I had no interest in actual rehabilitation, the insults and punishments that were thrown at me more or less rolled off my back, at least for a while. I did feel really sorry for most of the other patients, though; these people, the ones who genuinely wanted to get clean, didn't need to be yelled at and made to feel like pieces of dirt. They needed help, not harassment. The whole thing was just really, really depressing. I put in as many days as I could, but I didn't stay very long.

The second time I went to rehab, it was at a place called Bergen Pines County Hospital. The facility was a big building with two separate wings: one for alcoholics and one for drug addicts. Though I was both of those things by then, I checked in to the drug program because I really didn't think that drinking was a big deal. Back in the 1960s, and into the '70s, alcohol wasn't really a *problem*—at least not for young people. It was just something that everyone did; I was even told by the rehab counselors that alcohol was A-okay, as long as I stayed away from the drugs.

It seemed to me that only lonely, old men—the kind I pictured standing around a trash can fire, drinking ripple out of paper bags—went into treatment for alcohol, and I certainly didn't want to be stuck in that crazy place with a bunch of boozers. I wanted to be with the drug addicts. They were so much cooler to hang out with.

Once I was there, though, I found out that there were some seriously mentally disturbed patients in the drug wing—people who seemed to be battling demons much bigger than the little narcotics devils that followed me around. They roamed the halls like zombies, wearing helmets and banging their heads on the concrete walls. I shared a bedroom with five other people; I lay on my cot all night with one eye open, afraid that one of the crazies would try to jump me. The whole place was a nut house, something right out of *One Flew Over the Cuckoo's Nest*.

I didn't stay long at Bergen Pines. It was a scary place, and while I didn't think that any rehab could help me, I was positive that this one would not. Besides that, I just wasn't interested in being helped.

Chapter 8

My dad finally got a new job—at Westinghouse, one of the really big companies that still existed in Newark. Everyone knew someone who worked there; sometimes, entire families were employed at the enormous plant. I had aunts and uncles who had worked there for years; even my brother Nicky worked there for a while. There was a lot of nepotism going around.

Taking advantage of that, my dad got me a job, too, though I have to wonder why he did it—he had to know that I'd blow it somehow. Though I really wasn't interested in working at all, I took the job and even managed to show up most days. It was kind of like school—something to keep me busy, and at least I was getting paid for it. It was certainly a lot easier than breaking into luncheonettes.

I was placed in an office as a copier; my duties consisted of duplicating company papers, and that was it. I had to use those primitive copy machines with the fire underneath, which I used to heat up the cheese Danish I had every day for breakfast. I guess I didn't have a lot of respect for the tools of my trade, but I was actually pretty productive in the morning. Maybe that was because I knew that in the afternoon, nothing at all was going to get done.

The Westinghouse plant was right next door to the Seventh Avenue projects, where I went every day at lunchtime—sometimes alone, sometimes with a coworker named John—to buy dope and get high. The projects were a vile place to even visit, and I couldn't imagine living there. The hallways were filthy, the walls were disintegrating, the air just reeked of decay and misery, and the apartments themselves were usually not much better.

To get the drugs I wanted, I usually had to go into a dealer's home. Most of the guys I bought from were decent enough, all things considered; they definitely had the advantage when I went to see them, and none of them ever tried to get violent with me or anything. One guy was even nice enough to offer me some pizza along with my dope once, but when he opened the oven to show me what he was cooking, about a million roaches scurried out. "I think I'll pass," I said, shoving my purchase in my pocket and getting the hell out of there as fast as I could.

If I didn't shoot up right in the dealer's apartment, I'd go up to the projects' rooftop to take care of business. Then, I'd head back to work and disappear into the bathroom, only coming out if John ran in to tell me that someone was looking for me. Then, I'd go out in the office and he'd stay in the bathroom for a while, until someone came looking for him.

One afternoon, I was sitting on the toilet in a bathroom stall, nodding off from the high I'd caught at lunchtime. I had my elbows on my knees, and my face in my hands, and I was snoring away, blissfully unaware of anything that was going on anywhere else in the world.

All of a sudden, John ran in and pounded on the stall door, scaring me half to death. He said that Tony, our supervisor, was looking for me. Tony was actually a close friend of my family, so he really kept an eye on me. I jumped up and swung the door open—and then fell flat on my face. I didn't know it until I'd tried to put my weight on them, but both my legs had fallen asleep while I'd been sitting there. I had to lie on the bathroom floor until the numbness went away, and by time I got out to the office, thankfully, it was empty.

Tony had probably gone back to his own office to call my dad, which he did just about every day, to complain about me. "Where's Steve?" he would demand in his weird, high-pitched voice or, "What is that kid of yours *doing*?" Pretty much from the day I started, I had a lateness problem, and a problem with disappearing for extended periods of time. I feel bad that my dad got so harassed for my poor performance, but the situation was really good for me, and I hoped that it would last.

Before long, I found out that I didn't even have to go outside my job to score—I could get what I needed right there in the Westinghouse building. This was great, because those projects? Not exactly a safe place for a white kid to be hanging out. I also found out after a while that there was a drug store, around the corner from where I worked, where I could get my cough medicine. The pharmacist, of course, wouldn't sell me the stuff every day, but I was good at convincing coworkers to buy it for me. I had the longest-running nonexistent head cold in history, and every one of them bought it.

So, once I knew that I could get what I wanted at or close to work, I only had to go to the projects if I wanted heroin, and I still didn't love that stuff as much as my pills. If they were easy to get, I had no reason to go anywhere else.

Though I was, for the first time in my life, making a decent salary, I still never had any money on me. I borrowed from a guy in the company—a loan shark—to buy my drugs every day, and when I got my weekly paycheck, I cashed it and handed it over to him, to pay him back with interest. Then, I borrowed more money from him on the spot so that I could buy more drugs.

I worked at Westinghouse for a couple of years—*a couple of years*—before I was asked to leave. Though my lackluster performance hadn't seemed to faze my dad too much before that, my firing was tremendously embarrassing for him, and for the rest of my family who worked there. My Aunt Mary—Mom's sister—was especially annoyed by the situation because she was some sort of bigwig at Westinghouse. At least, that's what I'd heard; I never really knew what she did because I never took that much interest in anything going on around there.

Chapter 9

Though Dad continued to get me out of a lot of bad situations, and often saved me from facing the legal consequences to my actions, at home, he'd started to reach his threshold. He checked my pockets sometimes when I entered the house—looking for drugs, I guess, but he should've known I wasn't going to keep them anywhere he could find them. He tried to impose penalties on me for messing up—grounding me, restricting my activities— but it was far too late for that. I'd already been doing whatever I wanted for years, and *only* what I wanted, so his rules went in one of my ears and directly out the other. I just didn't listen to him at all, despite the many times he'd helped me get out of trouble. That's gratitude for you.

In one strangely misguided attempt to keep me on the straight and narrow, Dad bought me a car—a '65 Chevy that I tooled around Newark in. I crashed it a month after he gave it to me, while I was driving down McCarter Highway, where I hit a wall at a pretty high speed. I stumbled out with my chin bleeding and walked all the way home in a daze, then called the police to report the car stolen, just so I wouldn't have to deal with it anymore.

I don't know if I really have to say it again, but cops didn't care about *anything* back then, and they sure weren't running out the station door to find my Chevy and apprehend its supposed abductors. Hell, I could've called and said I was dead and they wouldn't have even looked for the guy who killed me. Eventually, I just went back to McCarter Highway and got my car. It was exactly where I'd left it.

My dad, being the good guy that he was and always on the

lookout for a way to set me on a good path, thought that maybe getting my car fixed up might help me out. He paid for the extensive repairs it needed—I tell you, running into a wall head-on is no joke—and I thanked him, and then went right back to tearing around the streets of our neighborhood.

Not much later, one night while I was driving home with a belly full of pills, cough medicine and vodka, the Chevy and I got into another scrape. This time, I skidded it right underneath a parked tractor-trailer. My car was completely totaled but miraculously, I was not. Though I'd hoped just a little bit that Dad would swoop in to rescue my vehicle again, he didn't this time, and that was the end of my illustrious career as a legitimate car owner.

My brother Nicky was a Newark policeman—I know, the irony is hysterical. We even slept in the same bedroom at our parents' house until Nicky got married and moved out. We never seemed to like each other, even as kids; Nicky was always a difficult guy to get along with, always angry, always violent. As we got older, he developed a personality with no compassion, no middle ground, no understanding. There was no gray area in any part of his life, whereas mine was nothing but. As you can imagine, I was an eternal thorn in his side. I embarrassed him—and everyone else I was related to—on a daily basis.

Nicky and I fought more than we didn't, and I threatened to take his gun and kill him in his sleep on more than one occasion—and I really meant to do it, too. For a long time, I really just hated the guy and his constant nagging. He was never at a loss for words when telling me all the ways in which I disappointed and embarrassed him and the rest of our family. He always said that I made him look bad at work, and I'm absolutely sure that he was right, but as you can imagine, I did not care.

Nicky worked at the police station in the North District in Newark, in the second precinct, where everyone who was arrested in that area was taken for holding. Not surprisingly, he was disliked by his peers. Simply by being who he was, with that unbending attitude, he alienated every one of his coworkers and I'm sure that a lot of the time, I suffered the consequences of his unpopularity. When the other cops from Nicky's precinct came across me on the street, whether I was doing something illegal or not, their eyes lit up; arresting me and beating me was a great way, to them, to get back at my older brother. Sure, I deserved it sometimes. But I know I definitely got some extra kicks in there, too, for reasons that were entirely not my fault.

There were a lot of people on the streets who hated Nicky just as much—criminals he'd busted, other folks he'd harassed—and between them and the other officers from the North District, I practically had to have eyes in the back of my head to survive. Thank God that I was able to handle myself, or I might not have made it out alive.

Time went on, and everything stayed pretty much the same in my life. The most important thing to me was staying high as much as possible, but sometimes, I didn't have the money or the means to get the pills and cough medicine that I needed to keep the party going. When that happened—when my body didn't get the fix it was expecting—I went through severe, painful withdrawal. I was in the throes of a serious, horrendous addiction that turned into a real monster when I didn't feed it on time.

One Christmas Eve, I was at home with my family, even though we were kind of ignoring the holidays in general; Mom was really sick by then and there was nothing festive about the season for any of us. For whatever reason, I ran out of my pills, and before I knew what was happening, I just couldn't move. My neck stiffened, and my hands curled up into petrified claws. I felt like I was slowly becoming paralyzed.

My uncle, who had been over at the house visiting, literally picked me up and put me in the car, and he and my dad drove me to an emergency room, where I was treated by a Dr. Friedman. He first asked what I'd been taking, and I told him that I'd been drinking cough medicine and popping pills for at least forty days straight. Without a word, without any sort of lecture or admonishment about the evils of drugs, he went and got a syringe and shot me up with a muscle relaxant. It was the greatest sense of relief I'd ever experienced. I felt renewed, and ready to go back out there and stock up on drugs so the same thing would never happen again.

Chapter 10

We'd all been preparing for my mother's inevitable death for a while, but when she finally passed on, it was still a blow and a shock and everything else that the loss of a close loved one was supposed to be. It wasn't sudden, and its cause wasn't anything mysterious, but knowing that she wasn't around anymore—even just not hearing her coughing from the bedroom—made the house feel empty.

At least, that was how it was for everyone else, for my brothers and Anne and Dad, and for the relatives and neighbors who seemed to be immediately knocking on our front door. For me, it was just like, I left home in the morning and she was alive, and when I came home in the afternoon, she wasn't. I walked into the house and Nicky simply told me, "Mom died," and that was that.

I went to my room to lie down. I stared at the walls for a while, trying to figure out how I should feel. She was only forty-nine years old; I was only nineteen; the whole thing was a tragedy. After a while, I tried to force myself to cry, because I knew it was what I was supposed to be doing, and it just wasn't happening on its own. My cousin Linda came in and sat down on my bed with me, and she rubbed my back, so I guessed that my attempt at mourning had been a success.

As people wandered quietly around my house, talking about my mother's funeral and burial arrangements in strangely hushed voices, like they were trying to keep it all a secret, I stayed in my room, lying on my bed for what seemed like (and might have been) hours. I was still wearing my coat, which concealed a freshly bought bag of pills and a bottle of cough medicine. I was dying for them; I clutched them in my fingers, inside my pocket, and thought of nothing but how and when I could to get them into my system. In all honesty, I was a little pissed off that my plans for the night had been ruined.

On the day of Mom's wake, my brother Nicky came downstairs dressed in his Sunday best, which included my favorite jacket. Well, let me back up a little bit: It was *his* jacket, but he had given it to me a while before. It was a nice coat, though I don't remember what color it was, or what the cut looked like. In fact, I don't think that I had even worn it once.

So, the reason why it was my favorite? It was where I hid my stash. The jacket had been hanging in my closet for months with my pills in its pockets, but otherwise gathering dust. Nicky had never made any mention of wanting it back, so when he showed up in our kitchen wearing it that day, I was pretty much taken by surprise.

First, I had a good laugh about it: Nicky the badass Newark cop, parading around with a pocketful of sleeping pills. But then, I lit into him—I had to have that jacket back right away. Of course, I couldn't tell him why, so when I tried asking him nicely, he basically told me to fuck off. Then, I yelled at him, and that didn't go over too well, either. Finally, we ended up in an all-out fistfight. He won, and he stormed out of the house, leaving for the funeral home with my jacket, and my entire stash, on his person.

At the wake, instead of being a good son and concentrating on really mourning the loss of my mother, my mind could not stop obsessing about those pills in Nicky's jacket. Grieving friends and relatives hugged me and kissed me, and talked to me about the lovely flowers and what a good woman my mother had been, and how much she would be missed, and I nodded and smiled at them while keeping one eye trained on my brother at all times.

At the moment, there was no bigger issue in my mind than getting those pills back. I'd been using for the better part of six years by then, and my body simply needed the stuff—*needed* it, not *wanted* it. I'd graduated to different drugs over time, each one worse than the last, but I always went back to those pills as my mainstay, and the thought of someone taking them away from me, even temporarily, set my mind on fire.

I stalked Nicky around the funeral parlor, keeping track of his every move, waiting for my chance. Finally, *finally*, when he took the jacket off and laid it across the back of a chair, I swooped in and stole my pills back, and everything in the world seemed right again. Oh, except that my mother was lying in a casket at the front of the room. I tried, from that point on, to focus more on the situation at hand.

As soon as the wake was over, I ran outside and right into the backseat of my friend's waiting car. The door was barely closed before I had pills in my mouth, and as we sped off, my mind finally relaxed, dreaming of whatever other narcotics we would ingest that night. The long, hard day was finally over, and I was ready for my reward for getting through it.

Chapter 11

I knew that my reaction to Mom's death was not right. I knew that I should feel more heartbroken, that I should miss her more. Maybe it was because I'd been raised to never let the things inside me come out; maybe I was just numb from the drugs. Whatever the cause, I was aware that something about my emotions was, in a word, fucked.

After she was buried, after she was gone for a while, Mom's absence began to weigh on me, little by little. The house really was different without her around. Everything went on pretty much as usual, but something was just *off* about the everyday routine. Dad tried his best to keep it all together, but I knew how hard it was for him. By then, it was only him, me and Anne left in the house, and he really, really missed Mom when she was gone.

In the middle of all this, I made my first honest effort at getting clean. Not for any real, conscious reason—not to honor my mother's memory, or to try to get my otherwise meaningless life together—but just because it was something to do. I was tired of people (Nicky, my dad) being on my back about it all the time, and I thought that maybe if I got clean and stayed that way for a while—not permanently, just for a while—they'd leave me the hell alone.

I'd been hearing about an experimental program in New Jersey called methadone maintenance, wherein I could go to a clinic and get some sort of liquid medication that would take the place of heroin or pills. Basically, I'd be trading one (illegal) addiction for another (government-approved) one. The point of the program was to give free narcotics to addicts, so we wouldn't have to go out and commit crimes to get what we needed. I figured that if I never had to claw my way out of another luncheonette in the middle of the night just for some spare change, I'd be happy enough.

To be admitted to the methadone program, you had to be at least twenty-one years old, but I was only nineteen at the time, so Dad signed me in. He gave his permission willingly—anything to try to get me on that right path, as usual—but neither one of us really knew what he was handing me over to.

First, I had to go into a rehab facility, a place called Skillman that wasn't in Newark but might as well have been for all the racial problems it had. It was just like being back in high school for me—everything was segregated by skin color, and it felt like the whole place could bust out into a riot at any moment. I'm not saying that I liked it there, but at least it was an atmosphere I understood.

As soon as I got to Skillman, they put me through a brutal detoxification process to get the drugs out of my system. I was tied down to a bed by my wrists and ankles for days, maybe weeks—I lost any sense of time I may have had once they put me in that room. The nurses kept a tongue depressor nearby, just in case, to shove in my mouth if I went into convulsions, and they fed me pills several times a day—Librium, to take the edge off the withdrawal. Even in my delirium, I was pretty sure that they didn't help one bit.

When that painful process was finally done, I was allowed to start taking the methadone, which had to be built up in my system very gradually. Every morning for three months, I got out of bed at five-thirty for my "medication"—the methadone liquid mixed into a cup of orange juice, with a little more of the former and a little less of the latter each time. The methadone itself had no taste or smell, but I knew that it was there because as soon as I swallowed my little cocktail, I had an immediate and overwhelming sense of well-being. Like I was floating on a goddamn cloud.

Remember that this methadone program was in its first stages—it was still deemed "experimental"—so the people running it really didn't know how much of the stuff a body could take, or how much one would need to function properly. Eventually, they had me up to a hundred and twenty-five milligrams of the stuff a day; currently, in 2007, the most a patient will get is thirty milligrams in a twenty-four-hour period. Like I said, it was experimental, and I guess you could say that I reaped the benefits of that.

Even without those facts and figures, while I was in the induction phase of the program, I knew that they were giving me way too much. After my dose, I couldn't do anything but sit, smoke and nod out all day long. It was pretty much what I'd been doing on the outside, except now, I had a comfy chair and a warm room to do it in, and everything was free. It was like heaven, and I wasn't about to tell them to cut back.

I was a zombie the entire time I was at Skillman. I did literally nothing, all day, every day. I did attempt to read a book that someone had given me, but over the course of my ninety-day stay, I didn't even make it to the bottom of the first page. That's how out of it I was.

After the methadone buildup was successfully accomplished, I was admitted into the maintenance program and released from Skillman. I was out on my own again, and every day, I had to go to a clinic to get the methadone I needed. I was assigned to one in Elizabeth, New Jersey—not too far from Newark—and when I showed up on my first day, I found that a few of my friends from high school were going there, too. Small world and all that. It was nice to see some familiar faces.

Chapter 12

Even aside from the little class reunion, the Elizabeth clinic was actually an awful lot like Baringer High, with a little Skillman thrown in for good measure. People shuffled around in the hallways, high out of their minds; the racial tension was incredibly thick, and the threat of sudden violence just hung in the air around us, waiting for an excuse to drop. Black patients and white patients had to go in separate doors, too, just like in the old times, so that we wouldn't, God forbid, see each other and be tempted to start a riot. The whole situation, I thought, was kind of funny. We were all adults there, but we were still treated like kids—a punishment that we probably deserved.

I met up with my old friends early each morning outside the clinic, where we'd hang around and bullshit for a while. Being in with the crowd again brought back a lot of memories, *and* a lot of the peer pressure I'd gone through earlier in my life, and before long, I was right back in the gang again, buying pills from the dealers that haunted the area around the clinic—yeah, so much for that whole "getting clean" thing.

After making our purchases, we'd head inside for our methadone. The rules said that when we were given our doses in the little plastic cups, we were supposed to drink them right in front of the clinic employee who'd administered them. The rules did not say, however, that we had to swallow, and those of us who had pills in our pockets soon became experts on how to hold the methadone mixture in our mouths until we got back outside, where we could use it to wash down our pills. Some people even spit their doses into bottles and sold them, and I'll admit that I paid for just such a thing from time to time, when I had the extra money.

The high that I got from the pills and the methadone together was tremendous. It lasted for a full twenty-four hours; it really kept me floating until the next morning, when I could come back and get more.

Because I was basically getting drugs that I liked for free, I kept up with the methadone program, but it didn't mean that I was a changed man. I was still my volatile old self, prone to fighting and unconcerned about the consequences of just about everything I did. I got into a confrontation at the clinic one morning, and along with a couple of my friends from Newark, I beat a guy up pretty badly. Why? I don't remember. Probably, I didn't like the way he looked at me, or the way he *didn't* look at me. I didn't need a whole lot of provocation back then to put a guy back in what I thought his place should be.

But because of that fight, the people in charge of the methadone program decided to kick me out, which was a complicated process. They couldn't just shove me out the door and say, "Nice knowing you, never come back." Instead, they had to send me to Skillman again, to take me off the methadone gradually over a long period of time, so I wouldn't go through withdrawal.

When I got to Skillman, I found out that there was a committee I could appeal to, some panel of people in charge who would listen to my story and decide if I should *really* be kicked out or not. I pled my case to them, and begged them to let me stay. I gave them every sob story I could think of to try to win them over. In the end, it worked: They agreed, and I was released from Skillman, and told to report to the Dana Clinic in Newark from then on.

Around that time, my sister, Anne, was dating a guy named Mike, who was a supervisor at Western Electric in Newark. Mike was a nice guy, even to me, and surprisingly, when he heard what I was going through with the methadone clinic, he offered to get me a job at his company. I guess he figured, good boy that he was, that he would lend me a hand on my way back up into the good graces of decent society.

Of course, all he was doing was giving me one more thing to pass the time during the day, a way to get some money to buy pills with. I was a total train wreck then, going to the methadone clinic early in the morning, scoring pills and then showing up at the job and doing absolutely nothing. I'd flop down at my desk at 8:00 and immediately go into a nod. The only thing that brought me back to consciousness was the lunch bell at noon.

Sometimes I hauled myself down to the cafeteria to eat with the other employees, none of whom I was interested in getting to know. One lunch hour, I was stuck at a table with some woman whose shrewish voice was cutting directly through the pleasant narcotic haze I had surrounded myself with. Something she said— could have been anything; could have been something totally innocuous—seemed really offensive to me, so I got up, jumped onto the table and grabbed her by the neck.

As I choked her, the cafeteria seemed to explode; everyone around us jumped to her defense, and one guy came up and hit me pretty hard. I kept on with the choking, wishing that the woman would just pass out and shut up already, but the others were pulling her out of my grasp and when it looked like the odds were no longer on my side, I ran out of the building, pissed off and formulating a revenge plan in my head.

From a pay phone outside, I called a couple of friends who I knew had nothing better to do, and they drove out to Western Electric to give me a hand. They pulled into the lot where I was hiding, and they parked their car; one of them took a big old lug wrench out of the trunk and gave it to me, and we just hunkered down and waited for the end of the workday.

At 5:00, the guy who had hit me during the cafeteria scuffle walked out with all his buddies, laughing and looking like he thought he was some kind of superhero. I snuck up behind him in the crowd, pulled back and let 'er rip, giving the guy one hell of a thump across the back of his head with my wrench. My friends started fighting with his friends, and the whole thing turned into a sort of mini-riot within minutes. We kept at it, beating the hell out of anyone we could get our hands on, until the cops came and broke it up.

In trying to sort out what had happened, the police questioned everyone on the scene. In line with the general code of the times, when they got to the guy I'd attacked, he didn't point his finger at me; back then, there was some sort of screwed-up honor in not ratting on your enemy. I was grateful, but at the same time, I really just wanted to hit him with the wrench some more.

Anyway, the cops guessed that I had started the whole thing, and I was arrested for assault. As usual, Dad took care of it, and nothing ever happened to me legally because of the incident. However, when I tried to go back to work at Western Electric, I was told quite firmly that my services there would no longer be needed.

Chapter 13

After getting fired, I guess I did some thinking about my life and myself, and for the first time probably ever, I felt a tiny bit like I should maybe start trying to do the right thing. What "the right thing" was, I had no idea—I'd never done it in my life. But, I tried to keep myself open to suggestions.

In lieu of any better ideas, for the time being, I continued on with the methadone program. I woke up and went to the clinic every morning and then went home, smoked cigarettes and watched *Green Acres* on TV. I became a huge fan of Arnold the Pig—sadly enough, seeing him was the highlight of my day.

I wasn't even taking pills anymore; the stuff they gave me kept me sufficiently high, and besides, I didn't have any money. Though I wasn't doing a damn thing with my life, I was doing everything that the program asked of me, and for the moment, that felt like enough, at least until something else came along. It may not have been the most productive lifestyle, but at any rate, I wasn't out robbing people anymore—which I guess made me a successful patient in the eyes of the experimental maintenance program.

When a guy I knew at the clinic offered me a job where he worked—at Foodtown, stocking shelves on an overnight shift—I gave it a shot. I needed to start getting out of the house more, to go somewhere other than the clinic, to do something that didn't involve methadone. The guy agreed to drive me to work and then to the clinic in the morning, since he was going there anyway, too.

And that was my life for a while: still sleeping during the day, but working at night and getting my methadone hit first thing in the morning. It was a routine, a mundane one, but I was good with that—it was something I could stick to. I didn't have to think too much about what I was doing; I could just go and do it. For the time being, it was exactly what I needed, and I found that I was good at it, too. I was a really hard worker, and I excelled at every task they gave me.

Then, one night, something out of the ordinary happened: A neighbor asked if I wanted to go out to a club. I hadn't been out socially in so long—it felt like I *never* had—so I figured, what the hell? What harm could one night out on the town do?

We ended up at a place called the Cus from Ho, in Ho-Ho-Kus, New Jersey, and that was where I met my future ex-wife, Debbie. She was standing at the bar with her friend Donna—the real object of my interest that night, if you want to know the truth. Donna was a tall brunette with a nice body, and I was really attracted to her, so I tried to chat her up. She was polite, but it was Debbie who was the real talker. She was very outgoing, aggressive even, and I really liked her style. From that night on, I guess you could say that we were inseparable.

After Debbie and I had been dating regularly for a little while, she brought me to meet her parents at their house in Monsey, New York. We stayed over for a weekend, and everything about the trip was an eye-opener for me. She came from such a *normal* family: Her parents were normal, they lived in a normal house, we ate meals together... For me, it was like being on another planet, one where mothers didn't get sick and fathers didn't get laid off from their jobs. This crazy thing I was thrown in the middle of, it was like the family I'd never had. It was like the family that I had almost forgotten was even possible.

Debbie was a good girl, and I was pretty sure that I didn't deserver her. If we had met a year earlier—or hell, a few months earlier—I was sure that she would have run in the other direction. But, she'd found me on an upswing, and so she didn't see me as the lowlife I had been. I wanted very much to keep it that way, so

I kept as quiet as I could about my past. She knew I was taking methadone, but that was the extent of my evils as far as she was concerned. Obviously, I really didn't tell her anything.

Debbie's father was a manager for Cadillac in New York, and like the others before—Dad, Mike—who had for some reason thought I might be a reliable employee, he got me a job, at a dealership in Newark. I started at the bottom, in the parts department, for very low pay, but I gave it my all anyway. I excelled even at that menial position, and endeared myself to all the higher-ups as quickly as I could; I was charming, I guess, and they liked that. I'm sure that all the years of bullshitting my way out of some intensely messed-up situations had something to do with it.

Though I'd quit the Foodtown gig some time before, I took on another part-time grocery store job to make ends meet, and because Debbie and I had started talking about getting married sometime in the future, and I knew that was going to be an expensive event. Each morning, I ran from the clinic to the dealership, and then to the food store after that. I put in long hours every day but was glad to be busy—all the work kept my mind off of the pills I wasn't taking. I guess you could say that work became my new drug of choice.

Once I got into this routine, I was feeling so good about myself, I decided that I would get off the methadone before my wedding day. I wanted to enter my marriage with a clear head, with nothing holding me back, but I didn't realize just how hard the detox would be.

I talked to the people at the Dana Clinic about it, and they agreed that I could be discharged from the program. Thankfully, I didn't have to check myself into Skillman again to get weaned off the stuff, though—they just lowered my dosage at the clinic every week, until I was down to nothing. At the end, I was just drinking plain orange juice.

Though I'd been through some monumentally shitty stuff in the past, getting off methadone was probably one of the most difficult things I had done up to that point. I was essentially going through withdrawal, same as it would be with any drug, but it took so long, dragged out over days and months, with just enough side effects to make me feel like I was slowly losing my mind. I didn't sleep for days on end, and being up all the time was just painful; my legs always hurt, my bones ached, even my hair didn't feel right. I lay awake in bed every night, staring at the ceiling and just wishing for some relief.

No, I didn't go back to the pills, or to heroin, or even to methadone, which was a miracle, really. I did start drinking alcohol again, but remember, that was no big deal back then. And it wasn't for fun; I just thought, in my ever-wakeful misery, that if I downed a bottle of wine, it would knock me out and I could finally sleep. I was desperate, and it worked, which of course meant that I would be trying it again, and again, and again.

Getting off methadone and still trying to maintain the rest of the decent life I'd been building for myself was very, very hard, but in the end, I did it, and I have to say that I was proud of myself. However, it left me with a new dilemma to consider: For the first time in my life, I was faced with the prospect of reality, with no narcotic crutches to lean on.

Chapter 14

Once I started to live what could be considered a normal life—or, at least, one that was not as degenerate as the one I'd led before—some very strange things started to happen. I started to feel *happy*. People were being *nice* to me, and I was being nice right back to them. Things just seemed to be falling into place, and I wondered why, if being *normal* made everything so easy, I hadn't done it much sooner.

Perhaps one of the strangest things of all was that I was doing really well at work. I excelled at my job, which I attributed to my addict's mentality. My smooth-talking skills were top-notch, honed over years of negotiating with drug dealers, cops and other criminals. I was an expert at figuring out what people wanted to hear, and then giving it to them, so that they would give me what I wanted: in this case, their money.

The Cadillac people seemed to like what I was doing—the money and promotions they threw at me made that pretty clear. I was also sure I was doing something right just based on the number of outside job offers I got. The further I moved up the corporate ladder, the more the other companies came knocking, wanting me to go run their parts departments.

Because I felt no loyalty whatsoever toward the company that had given me my first big break in the industry, I regularly entertained offers from its competitors. One day, I got a particularly good bid from a General Motors rep who had come in to the dealership to meet me. He told me that if I'd go work at a Chevrolet place in South Jersey, he'd give me a demo car, and a considerable amount of money. He'd even make me the boss of the place.

The boss, I thought. That was some amazing shit. I accepted his offer on the spot and immediately quit my night job at the grocery store.

At Chevrolet, I did make more money, and I did run the show. But, I also worked long hours and had a hell of a commute. By the time I got home at night, I was exhausted—a welcomed change from my sleepless methadone withdrawal period, but a drag nonetheless. Most nights, it was all I could do to knock back a few drinks and shuffle off to bed, so I could get a few hours of sleep, wake up the next morning and do it all over again.

During my time at Chevrolet, I really managed to build up my reputation in the automobile industry. I worked harder at that job than I had at anything before in my life, and I found that with that diligence came some nice rewards. There were sizable bonuses and shiny new cars. I even won trips, because of my high sales numbers, to Hawaii and Switzerland—places that may as well have been on another planet for a guy from Newark like me. Before then, the only islands I'd ever been to were Long, Staten and Riker's.

This sort of recognition really filled me with a sense of self-importance that I had been missing my whole life. For once, I wasn't being valued because I could drink a lot or because I got all crazy in a fight. My worth was estimated by how much money I made and how far up the corporate ladder I climbed. People actually respected me. It was like I was living the life I would have all along, had it not been for the narcotics.

In addition to all this newfound success, Debbie and I finally got married. I was 25 years old, and felt like I was on top of the world. We bought a house in Bloomfield, New Jersey, a decent, suburban town, and started in on making our own family; in time, we had two beautiful daughters. I had no skill at being a husband and father, but I tried my best. And even with the shortcomings that I did have, I still felt like I was at the top of my game. I felt good about myself for the first time in my life.

When I say that work was a substitute drug for me, I'm not kidding. I wasn't shooting up or swallowing pills anymore, but I was spending 12 hours a day at my job, sometimes seven days a week, even though no one told me that I had to. Something in my head just told me that nothing was as important as staying at the dealership until everything was in order, and exactly the way I wanted it. As with everything else in my life that was bad for me in some way, I took my job to the extreme and dedicated just about every waking moment to it.

Because I worked so much, I got physically run down sometimes. I was never one to take care of my health anyway, so when my body had enough, it really let me know. Nothing *too* serious— just a cold, or a stomach bug—but enough to make me feel like staying in bed for a few days would be just fine.

But of course, I couldn't miss work. Never, *never* could I miss work. In the absence of any addictive substances in my system, I had my job to fall back on, and I clung to it like a life raft; with nothing else to keep me moving day in and day out, I depended on stress and overtime too as a substitute high. I *needed* to go to work.

So, one winter day, when I was getting knocked out by a particularly bad flu, I packed my two young daughters into the car and headed downtown, to a local drug store, to find some relief. I was perusing the over-the-counter cold medicines and coughing my lungs out when the pharmacist came up to me.

"Forget about those," he said. My wife and I were regulars there, and this guy always treated us well. "They don't work. Let me give you something better. All you have to do is sign for it."

I looked at him for a moment, my brain flashing back to all those times in high school when I'd traveled all the way to New York City to get cough medicine that I had to sign for. *How come I never knew this guy was here?* I thought, and I smiled at him. "Sounds good," I said, trying not to hack on him. "Show me what you've got."

Back out at the car, I bundled my girls back into their car seats, and then sat down behind the wheel. I opened up the bag the pharmacist had given me and slowly withdrew its contents: a bottle, dark brown glass, with a child safety cap. I unscrewed it and without even bothering to read the label, I put it to my lips and knocked the entire thing back.

When the bottle was empty, I held it out in front of me and let out a big, satisfied sigh. I stared at the label then, reading its words without comprehension, as though they were in a foreign language. "Don't drive while using this medication," it warned me. "May cause dizziness." My stomach began to turn, surprised by the sudden invasion of the sticky-sweet liquid, but everything else in my body was buzzing. Every limb, every hair, every cell was remembering this long-lost sensation, and thanking me for bringing it back.

I tossed the bottle onto the floor, started the car, and pulled out into the traffic of the busy downtown street. Driving home, I had only the vaguest awareness that I had done something wrong, or that there had been a bomb lying dormant inside of me, and that I had just lit the fuse.

Chapter 15

I went back to that drug store every three days for the next few months, complaining of a cough that I just couldn't seem to shake. When the pharmacist seemed to be onto my scam, I started sending my wife, but then he wouldn't give the medicine to her, either. So, I just moved on to other pharmacies. Most of the time, when I could, I brought my daughters with me to buy the stuff. For some reason, people seemed to look at me less suspiciously when I was carrying a baby in each arm.

At the time, none of this seemed at all weird to me. I wasn't alarmed that I was slipping back into a bad habit. I didn't really think that I was doing anything *wrong*. It was just a bottle of cough medicine once in a while, that I drank down in my basement workshop. After I chugged the whole thing, I'd turn the empty bottle upside down, so I'd have an extra mouthful in the cap later on, and store it in a cabinet. I had a nice collection going. *What on earth,* I said to myself over and over again, *could that possibly hurt?*

After I'd been at the Chevy dealership for some time, I got a tip that there was a Cadillac place in Clifton—much closer to home—that was looking for a manager. I jumped at this opportunity and called right away to set up an interview, which actually turned out to be totally unnecessary: On the day I went to meet with the owner, he took one look at my employment record and the recommendations I had from other people in the industry, and hired me on the spot.

I took this new position very seriously, and I worked even harder there, really busting my ass to be the best in the business. I even wore a jacket and tie every day, to give that extra impression of respectability. It didn't matter to me if I really *was* respectable, as long as I *looked* like I was.

To get through what turned out to be a really stressful employment situation, I continued on with the cough medicine habit. I had a driver at the company who went out to different pharmacies for me every day; he was a Spanish guy, and didn't speak English too well, so I'd just write him a note that he could hand to a pharmacist, detailing exactly what I wanted. The driver really didn't even know what he was buying. *All part of the job*, I figured, when I figured anything about it at all. Mostly, I just drank the stuff and didn't think about much else.

If I wanted to rationalize it, though, I easily could have: The cough medicine was a sedative, and something I certainly needed to deal with the level of stress associated with my job. There was a lot of pressure on me at work, a lot of people looking to me for answers, and I needed an outlet every now and again. Toward that end, I went out to a lot of lunches, too, with bosses, clients and the like; I would stay out for hours, schmoozing and drinking, and I'd go back to the office wasted. It was amazing I got anything done some days, but in spite of myself, I had enormous sales figures and earned huge bonuses. Everyone at Cadillac knew me and loved me. There was nothing—*nothing*—that I could do wrong.

Riding high on my own self-importance, I wasn't really concerned that I'd slipped back into my old, bad habits, and I really wasn't surprised, either, when I picked up some new ones, too. Cocaine, at the time—back in the late 1970s and early '80s—was just coming onto the scene. It was a recreational party drug; there was no shame in using it, and it wasn't considered addictive. People sniffed up lines of it right out in the open—at bars, clubs, sometimes even at work—and no one thought much of it.

Given my history of being unable to say "no," when someone I knew offered me some cocaine one night, you can bet I snorted it right up. And just as it had been with the cough medicine way back when, and the sleeping pills after that, and then the heroin, I immediately liked it, and I wanted to do it more. At no time did I think that I *shouldn't*; at no time did I think that it was wrong. To me, it was just a good way to keep me going, to keep me humming and buzzing and not having to think too much about anything.

Before long, I was using cocaine every single day—sometimes multiple times a day. I did it at work and when I was out at night; eventually, I even started bringing it home. I'd sit in my house and consume massive quantities of the stuff, getting zoned out of my mind and not sleeping at all. The fine line between "this is fun" and "this is painful, sick and wrong" was sometimes hard for me to find.

So as always, I went back to what had worked for me in the past. Hoping that a little extra liquor would help me sleep, I upped my alcohol intake—with cocaine in your system, you can drink almost double the amount that you could normally, so I really had to down an awful lot to feel any effect. In my methadone days, a bottle of wine had done the trick and sent me off to blissful slumber. To combat the cocaine, it was vodka by the gallon, straight up.

A lot of the time, I didn't know whether I was coming or going, awake or asleep. I snorted cocaine and got too high, and then I drank to bring me back down. I was like Alice, living in Wonderland: One made me big, one made me small. And I needed them both to balance each other out.

In the middle of all this mess, I brought back another of my old standbys: my lack of conscience. Whereas I used to break into stores, rob people and get into fights with no feelings of guilt at all, now, being the big shot family man and businessman that I was, I didn't resort to such base criminal activities.

Now, instead, I did things like taking my baby daughters along when I went to buy cocaine. I put them in their seats and let the car rock them to sleep while I drove through the worst neighborhoods in the state, getting what I needed from the worst lowlifes you could imagine. Did I stop and think, *Maybe I shouldn't be doing this*? Did I ever consider that maybe *I* was a lowlife myself? Of course I didn't. All I thought about was getting that white powder up my nose, and quick. I actually thought I was being a responsible father, because at least I wasn't leaving them home alone, like the pathetic junkies I'd see on the news, hand-cuffed and crazy looking as the words "child endangerment charges" flashed across the screen. That, I was sure, would never, ever be me.

Chapter 16

When I wasn't getting high out of my mind in the comfort of my own home, I was out at the clubs, doing the same thing. I was a regular at Chicago's in Lodi, some Latin clubs in New York, and Ashley's in Clifton. I stuck to the places where I was recognized, and regarded as a big shot, because I had to keep my inflated sense of self-worth going. Wherever I was—work, home, play—I had to feel like the most important person in the room or it all meant nothing, and I didn't need any reminders about how worthless I really was.

At the clubs, I always had a flock of young women around me, which I'm sure had *nothing* at all to do with the cocaine and money I threw around. Whatever the reason, I ate up the adoration and asked for more, and I probably could have had my pick of the girls and done whatever I wanted with them. I was like a high roller, a man about town, and everyone, I thought, wanted a piece of me.

But instead of hitting on a hanger-on, instead of going for one of those girls who fell at my feet every night, I set my sights on Donna, one of the hostesses at Ashley's. I watched her work all the time and I thought she had a lot of class about her. She was young and beautiful, and she was always so nice to me. She was nothing like my wife, who had just had two babies and wasn't in the best shape of her life, physically or mentally. Cruel, I know, but it's how I felt at the time.

My big shot brain told me that I should have Donna on my arm, that she would look good driving around with me in my brand-new Cadillac. I always had a top-of-the-line car; I was an important man in the company—I couldn't be seen in anything less. So, I pursued Donna, and even though she was engaged to an attorney at the time, I won her over. I stole her away from that perfectly upstanding citizen and pulled her down into my own world, like a caveman dragging his conquest home by the hair. I don't know what on earth she saw in me then, but she willingly entered into a relationship with me when what she should have done was run the other way. She was such a smart girl. She should have seen that I was a disaster waiting to happen.

In the middle of all this, my father started having health problems. Because of some pains in his chest, his doctor recommended heart bypass surgery, and during the operation, they found a cancerous spot on his lung. There were also complications afterward, and the doctors had to go back in to fix something in his chest; Dad's body was very traumatized, and he never fully recovered from the ordeal.

In the years after Mom's death, Dad had remarried—a woman named Mary, whom he worked with at Westinghouse. She looked exactly like Mom, and she took care of him like I imagined Mom would have, if things had been different. After his surgery, Dad did little else besides sit on the couch and stare off into the distance, until finally, he just gave up and passed away.

In keeping with my personal tradition, instead of bucking up and being a good son upon the death of my parent, I simply kept on being myself and not giving a shit. I don't remember much about my father's wake, because I was doing coke in the bathroom through most of it. For the few minutes I was out in the general population, I was drinking from a flask and trying not to have flashbacks of my mother's funeral. I was totally useless to everyone else, and I didn't care. That's just who I was at the time.

To keep myself going on this long downward spiral, I continued going to clubs almost every night, and getting more and more involved with Donna, the hostess from Ashley's. When I saw her—okay, and pretty much at all other times—I had absolutely no regard for the fact that I was a husband and father; to me, that was like some other guy, living some other life, and I barely knew him.

I guess that on some level, I wanted to get out of my marriage, but I wasn't strong enough, or *decent* enough, to talk to Debbie about a divorce. Instead, I took what I saw as the easier way out: I made her hate me. Granted, she didn't have far to go in that area, but I sure pushed her right over the edge, every chance I got.

The drinking, the drugging, the clubbing—it was all weighing on her by then, and I just made it worse by picking fights with her over any stupid little thing I could. It wasn't because I was mad at her, or because she was even doing anything wrong. I just knew that if we argued good and loud, then I could storm out of the house in a fit of righteous indignation, without having to explain where I was going. And I did this just about every night.

After a few months of this routine, I got tired of it. One night, when we got into another big fight, I packed a few of my things and told Debbie that I was going away for a few days. After those few days were over, I never went back. The wife, the kids—I felt like they were dragging me down, and ruining all the fun I was trying to have on my own. I moved in with one of my assistant managers from work, and I brought Donna there to stay with me most nights, and I thought it was a great improvement in my lifestyle. Not once did it cross my mind that I had abandoned my family, and that maybe that wasn't such a good thing to do.

The way I saw it, I had just freed myself of some things that I shouldn't have had in the first place. A wife? Babies? A house in the suburbs? What had I been thinking? A guy like me didn't need stuff like that—not when there were parties to go to, and women to meet, and drugs to take. I felt like I'd been living with a mask on my face, and I'd finally taken it off. My family and everything about the good life I had built were dead to me. It was the trade off, I figured, for being free.

Chapter 17

So it was a Saturday morning, a little after sunrise. I had just come home—well, to my assistant manager's apartment, my halfway home at the time—and flopped down on the couch, ready for some serious shut-eye, as soon as I could stop the room from spinning around me. *Another good night at the clubs*, I thought with a slow smirk, remembering the highlights of an evening that had been filled with all the things I loved the most: coke, booze and women.

In the middle of my sleepy reverie, the phone started to ring. *Who the FUCK is this?* I thought, wishing that I could grab it from where I was—not to answer it, but to pull its cord right out of the wall. But, it was across the room and way out of reach, so with a big sigh, I rolled off the couch and stumbled over to it, barely able to see my way because of the bright sunlight coming in through the windows.

"Hello," I mumbled when I picked up, and then pulled the receiver away from my ear like the thing was on fire. A man's voice screeched at me from the other end of the call; it felt so loud, it made my brain hurt. I listened to the voice chatter on for a minute, and then put the phone's earpiece back to my head. "Who the fuck are you?" I asked, cutting the guy off mid-sentence.

He told me that he was my tenant—the guy who rented the second floor of my house in Bloomfield. The house I no longer lived in. The house where my forgotten wife and daughters resided. Did he not realize, I wondered, that I hadn't been around there for months? And wouldn't it have been easier for him to take his complaint right downstairs, to someone who might have actually given a shit?

59

Apparently, it wouldn't have; he wanted to talk to me, and me alone. He went on and on about how there was a leak in his roof, and how all his stuff was getting wet, and how I had to get it fixed a.s.a.p., and blah, blah, blah—I tuned him out after about ten seconds of it. He sounded mad, and maybe I should have been concerned, but my head was pounding, and his whiny voice was only making me feel worse. I rubbed my temples, squeezed my eyes shut, and managed to get out a quasi-sympathetic grunt every now and then, whenever it seemed appropriate.

I guess that wasn't the kind of response he wanted, though, because before long, he resorted to calling me names. I let him go on for a while longer, let him get out all he wanted to say, and when he finally stopped to take a breath, I very calmly asked, "Can you hold on for just a minute?"

Without even waiting for him to answer, I put the receiver down on the table, next to the phone's base, and slowly, calmly, walked back out of the apartment. I then got in my car and drove off, radio blaring, the sun beating down on my already exhausted head.

When I got to the house in Bloomfield, I walked up to this guy's door, whistling a happy tune. I rang the bell once—didn't want to seem too pushy—and waited with a smile on my face for him to open up. When he did, I laughed a little at how surprised he looked, and then, I punched him hard, directly in the face.

He reeled back and clapped his hands over his busted nose, trying to contain the blood that was gushing out of it like lava from Mount Vesuvius. He tried to retreat back into the house but before he could get away, I grabbed him by whatever I could get a hold of—shirt, hair, who knows—and dragged him down the stairs.

Once we reached the front lawn, I threw the guy down on the ground and kicked him, as hard as I could, over and over. He started to scream, which drew my wife and daughters outside, and then they were screaming, too. I ignored all the noise and just kept kicking.

And then, the cops showed up. I didn't know who'd called them, but they came out for me in full force, sirens wailing and lights blazing. I stood there on the lawn, still burying my foot in my tenant's ribs, breathing heavily, my head pounding, and waited for the battle to begin.

The officers got out of their cars—I heard the shuffling and the doors slamming. "Hey," I heard one of them say somewhere in the background. "I know him. He's a friend of mine."

And then there were hands on my shoulders, and the cops were pulling me off the guy I was beating to a bloody pulp. I kept kicking as they pulled me away, so focused on what I was doing that I barely had any idea what else was going on.

"Hey," the cop said again. "Steve."

I stopped and looked at him. Blinking a few times, my wits came back to me. I glanced at the tenant, rolling around on the grass, moaning and crying and clutching at his stomach.

"Hey," I said back to the officer, who was releasing his grip on my arm. I smiled a little, realizing that this sticky situation was just about to turn strongly toward my advantage. "How's your car running?"

As it turned out, almost all of these cops drove Cadillacs that I had sold them, and what was supposed to be a bust turned quickly into a reunion. The cops talked to the guy I'd assaulted, calmed him down and somehow, convinced him not to press charges against me. Maybe they promised that his roof would get fixed, though I knew that if it came to that, I sure as hell wasn't going to do it. I'd sooner come back and pick up kicking his ass right where I had left off.

Chapter 18

Working at Cadillac, I met people from all walks of life: big people, important people, people with lots of money. Some of them were on the level—real fine, upstanding citizens who just happened to enjoy driving expensive automobiles and exchanging favors with me once in a while, like the pharmacist who let me pick stuff off his store's shelves in return for replacing the wheels that had been stolen off his car.

Others, though—well, let's just say that some of them were not the kind you'd take home to meet your mom. I'm talking about hard guys, tough guys, intimidating criminals and manipulative mobsters who commanded respect and got whatever they wanted. And these were not just customers of mine, but colleagues, and guys I considered friends.

I can see now, though, that in reality, I was just another guy for them to use, a cokehead they suckered into doing their shady work for them. I did a lot of running around for these people; delivering drugs, collecting money, standing behind them and trying to look mean while they roughed people up—whatever tasks they assigned me, I happily did. Why? Because I wanted to be big like them. I wanted people to respect me, and to fear me, and hanging out with this deadly element put me, I thought, on a higher level of the social order, with more credibility. I thought that because I worked for mobsters, I was one myself.

However, big shot that I was, I still slept on my assistant manager's couch every night, and this did not exactly lend itself to the man-about-town image I was trying to project. Besides, I had started to feel like my welcome there was wearing itself out, so I found an apartment to rent by myself in Nutley, not far from where I worked. I called the place the Passion Pit—it was a real swingin' bachelor's pad, as they used to say, and I had big plans for using my newfound privacy to its fullest. I outfitted the joint in style, with shag carpeting so thick, I think a couple people got lost in there and were never found. I also bought a fifty-inch TV, the biggest one available back in 1980; they had just come on the market, and having one was some kind of status symbol.

The Passion Pit was a busy place from the get-go. There were always people at my door—college kids buying coke, mob guys collecting their money, and more women than I knew what to do with, including my old standby Donna and a couple of her friends. Some nights, I'd even drop her off at home when I was done with her and then head to a club to pick up another girl. In my mind, I was a real playboy, but now I can see that my luck with the ladies probably had more to do with the cocaine I gave them and less to do with my suave demeanor. Coke was a hot drug; everyone wanted some, and I had plenty to go around.

I liked the stuff an awful lot myself, too, but it wasn't my only vice. I was still drinking a lot, and I guess you could say that I also dabbled in gambling, though in an unlikely and somewhat unglamorous form: lottery scratch-off tickets. They'd just started selling them in New Jersey and once I got hooked on them, I started buying a few hundred dollars' worth at a pop. I'd sit at my kitchen table with this long string of tickets, a gallon of vodka and a pile of coke; I'd do a line, scratch a ticket and take a gulp of vodka and think, *Man, life just doesn't get any better than this.*

I was doing this little routine one night, drinking and sniffing and scratching, with some really, *really* good cocaine that I'd managed to get my hands on. It wasn't the typical street stuff, but Miami or Colombian; I had my own scales and had cut it all myself. I'd been at it for maybe an hour already and was bending over for another snort when I felt a weird pang in my chest, an odd racing of my heart that didn't hurt, but didn't feel entirely normal, either. In mid-lean, I looked down and saw that my rib cage was expanding and contracting with the force of my heart's beat. The damn thing was practically jumping out of my chest.

I stood up fast, knocking my chair over, and ripped off my shirt like I was the Incredible Hulk, suddenly feeling sweaty and hot and clammy all at once. I let out a strangled yelp as words like *heart attack* and *stroke* ran through my brain, sure that one or the other of them was going to take me down at any moment as a final reward for all the years I'd spent pumping my body full of illicit chemicals. "Shit," I yelled, looking around me frantically for something that would make this nightmare stop. "Shit!"

Because I had no better ideas about what might save my life, I flung open the apartment door and ran outside into the winter cold. I stood there in the icy wind, sweaty and shirtless, gasping for breath, my eyes tearing. I looked down at my violently thumping heart once again and thought, *That's it, I did it.* I looked around at the apartment's parking lot, at my big, fancy Cadillac that I would never get to drive again, and waited for something to happen. Waited for the end to come.

But then, just as suddenly as it had started, it all stopped. My heart returned to its normal, softer pace, and I stopped sweating. As the panic that had overtaken me receded, I sucked in a long, deep breath and blew it out slowly; apparently, I was no longer about to die, and everything slowly returned to normal.

I shook my head and went back into the apartment. "Almost really did it this time," I said as I got a towel from the bathroom and dried myself off. I put on a nice, warm sweater and threw out the shirt that I'd ripped off in the kitchen. I tidied up a little to get my mind off what had happened—threw away my losing scratch-off tickets and empty vodka bottles, brushed away some loose powder that had strayed from my gigantic bag of cocaine—and then I sat down at the table and did another big, fat line. I deserved it, I figured, for managing to stay alive.

Chapter 19

Every night of every week, I was going to a different nightclub. Or, rather, I had a rotating schedule of attendance that I followed like it was the Ten Commandments. On Mondays and Wednesdays I was at one place, Tuesdays and Fridays another; still another was set aside only for Thursdays and Saturdays. I followed such a regular routine that if anyone had wanted to kill me—and probably, *someone* did at one time or another—I would have been a really easy mark. Luckily, I partied with cops, mob guys, and everyone in between, so if anyone *had* tried to mess me up, they probably would have had quite a problem on their hands.

Ashley's, the club where I'd met Donna, was still one of my usual haunts—not because I was a great dancer or because I found disco music so appealing, but because the place was a good ego boost. All the regulars there knew me and for some reason, a lot of them looked up to me. I was a big shot, someone everyone wanted to know. I wasn't as big as the many mob guys who hung out there, too, but I *thought* I was. In my estimation, there was no one cooler in the world than Stephen Della Valle at that moment in time, and that self-confidence seemed to be enough to make people love me.

As I immersed myself in this sea of strangers and wallowed in all their shallow, sycophantic adoration, though, one thing still tied me to the shore of reality: my wife. For some reason that I could not for the life of me figure out, she'd started trying to get me to come back to her. She called me all the time, sometimes yelling and cursing, sometimes talking to me really sweetly, but always hounding me about my responsibilities toward her and our daughters, and reminding me of the good times we'd had and of how much my little girls missed me. On days when she felt particularly frustrated, she even had the girls call me themselves and ask in their tiny, bubbly voices, "When are you coming home, Daddy?"

But none of it worked. Whether she was nice to me or not, my wife was nothing but a thorn in my side, and I really just wanted her to leave me the hell alone. I was always rude to her when she called, and never gave in to any of her pleas or demands, and after a while, I guess that she got the hint. She just stopped calling.

Without a family, I could do whatever I wanted with the money I made. I got good paychecks from Cadillac and had wads of extra cash from my side job; I should've been living a pretty high life, wearing expensive suits and investing in the stock market, lying around in my posh home, surrounded by expensive artwork and the latest high-tech gadgets. I should have had it all.

But, just the opposite, I always felt like I was broke. I paid the rent on my small apartment each month, and whatever other bills were due, and after that, pretty much every dollar I earned went right into the hands of drug dealers, and then directly up my nose. After a while, I barely even had enough funds to make ends meet; cocaine was an expensive habit, a nasty, feral pet that had to be fed regularly and repeatedly, and it was chewing my wallet to shreds.

So, I had to come up with something new, some different way of getting the extra money I needed to keep my lifestyle alive. I didn't have any family members I could ask for money—or, at least, none that would give me any, if I did ask—and trying to get a loan, either from a bank or my mobster pals, would have been useless because I never would have been able to pay it back.

But there was one thing I could do. It came to me at work one day as I sat in my office, watching my employees running around, the whole place full of customers. The dealership had become very successful—thanks to me, I thought—and no one questioned anything I did there. I ordered enormous shipments of parts, went out and bought new delivery trucks, spent the company's money entirely at my own discretion, and no one batted an eye because for all I spent, I was bringing in five times as much. Whatever I did there worked out, and everyone knew it. I was golden.

"Misappropriation of funds" was what it was called in the legal system, this genius plan of mine, but to me, I was just skimming a little off the top here and there. I knew my business inside and out, and I knew just where to find the extra money that no one would miss. As the boss, I could manipulate the figures and keep it all covered up, and I believed that no one would be the wiser because I was so over-the-top confident in myself. I really thought that no one would ever find out. I thought I was entirely above reproach, and that I somehow deserved the extra money for all the hard work I did for the company.

Chapter 20

The problem with my plan? Once I put it into motion, I could never, ever take another day off from work for fear that someone would find out what I was doing. Having the extra money did solve some of my problems—with it, I could afford to pay for my rent, bills and food *and* for my drugs, alcohol and other nightlife expenses—but at the same time, I had to be on guard twenty-four hours a day. At the dealership, I became super-micromanager, always aware of where everyone was and what they were doing. Maybe it was just the proverbial cocaine paranoia, but I really felt for a while like I had to have eyes in the back of my head to keep the whole scam going.

And none of this did anything good for my already shitty sleeping habits. The constant worrying that someone would find out what I was up to, and the hypervigilance it took to keep it concealed, kept my brain churning nonstop, even into the small hours of the night, when I should have already been passed out in a lovely narcotic coma. A few months after I started stealing from my job, I felt like I hadn't had a good night's rest in years, and it showed—I was losing weight, the bags under my eyes could have held their own ZIP codes, and I had frequent nosebleeds from all the coke I was doing to keep me up and running. On some level, I was bizarrely okay with all of this; there was something about the sensation of always *going*, of always being on the move, that I liked sometimes. At the very least, it kept me from stopping and thinking too hard about how fucked up I'd become.

On nights when I really just had to get some shut-eye, I'd pop a couple Valium to knock me out for a few hours. I'd wake up in the morning still feeling like hell, so I'd hit the cocaine right away, to put everything back on track, and then later go out for a three-hour liquid lunch to bring me down again to the normal, zombie-like level at which I functioned best. It was a hell of a way to live.

Even with all my addictions, even with the cocaine craziness and the paranoia that only an embezzler can relate to, I moved up steadily in my job. In the short time I'd been in the auto business, I'd achieved more milestones than people who'd worked for the company their whole lives, and eventually, I worked my way up to number one in sales at Cadillac. I accomplished this because I'd always been really good at talking people into doing what I wanted them to; I was charming, as most addicts are when they want something, and I had a long list of faithful clients, with new ones coming in every day.

The company higher-ups continued to recognize my out-standing bullshitting skills and awarded me often, with prizes like exotic vacation packages—European resorts, remote islands, all sorts of places that I would have loved to visit, especially for free. Unfortunately, I never used any of them because a week away from my office meant five million opportunities for someone to find out about my secret relationship with the company's money.

So I soldiered on day after day, week after vacationless week, a slave to my job and even more so to my criminal activities. Some days, I was so shot from the sheer stress of it all that I should have stayed home to recover, but I hauled my groggy ass out of bed and went into the dealership anyway, just to keep an eye on my files. On days like that, I'd sit behind my desk for hours on end, spac-ing out, physically there but mentally on another planet, letting my employees cover for me. It was a wonder that any of them stayed working for me as long as they did.

On other days, when I was feeling more like the important, in-charge guy that I thought I was, to make up for the time I couldn't take off, I went on extended lunch hours with the other managers and returned to the dealership completely looped. I went on golf outings with the GM bigwigs, who seemed to enjoy having me along even though I regularly massacred the sport and the lawn it was played on. I puffed myself up and paraded around the dealership like the biggest bird in the roost, not even letting the owner of the dealership tell me what to do. One time, around Christmas, I had a falling out with him and when he then invited me out to dinner—letting bygones be bygones, I suppose, in the spirit of the season—I told him, "I don't break bread with assholes." Amazingly, he didn't fire me on the spot.

But to me, that made perfect sense. I was bigger than him, bigger than anyone and everything; I would never get *fired* like some normal person. I ran that dealership. I had women falling at my feet. I walked into restaurants, and people at other tables paid my bills. I was a mobster, a gangster, the master of all I surveyed and the pilot of my own destiny; the problem was that my plane was just about to fly into the side of a mountain, and I was flirting with the stewardess instead of paying attention to the lights and buzzers that announced my impending demise.

Chapter 21

The freshly waxed hood of my brand-new Oldsmobile Toronado gleamed in the sunlight as I raced down Route 3 in northern New Jersey, en route to see a man about a thing—the man being an Italian, and the thing being some cocaine he was going to sell me. It was the middle of a workday, and there was no traffic to speak of, so I jumped over to the left lane and floored the gas pedal, just to see how fast the car could go.

The car was a dream to drive, fast or slow, there was no doubt about that. It had a new Bose radio system, a beautiful leather interior, custom tires and wheels and a custom chrome grill. It was probably the nicest demo I'd driven to date. In my mind, it was just further proof that the company I worked for loved me: no crappy, used promotional cars for me, not ever. I told them I only wanted the newest and the best, and they made sure that I got it.

Arriving at my destination—a bar called JP's—I carefully positioned my car out in front, making sure not to get too close to any other cars; didn't want dings on the bumpers or nicks in the paint because of some other asshole who couldn't park. As I headed inside the building, I looked back over my shoulder at the Toronado and almost smiled at the damned thing. The car was so beautiful, such a good-looking automobile, and it made me happy knowing that it was mine, at least for the time being. I hated to leave it alone even for a few minutes.

Inside, I met up with a group of guys, three or four in all, friends of my mobster friends. We chatted and had a few drinks, then completed our transaction and shook hands. I turned around and left, purchase in hand, anxious to get behind the wheel of my new favorite toy once again.

When I hit the sidewalk, though, I stopped short. "What?" I said, confused by the gaping hole where my beloved car used to be. "The fuck?"

I scanned the area, looking up and down the street quickly, thinking that maybe I'd just parked it somewhere else without realizing it. *Maybe the few drinks I had are playing tricks on me*, I thought, trying desperately to make light of the situation. But after a fast inventory of everything in front of me, I had to admit that I wasn't in the wrong spot, and neither was my car. It was just gone. Disappeared. Stolen right out from under my nose. I swore on the spot that if I found the lowlife who had done it, I would fucking kill him.

I ran back into the bar and called the Clifton police, where I knew a bunch of guys who could help me out. They came over and helped me fill out a report, and then gave me a ride back to the dealership, where I informed the owner that my car had been stolen. He quickly gave me a replacement, which put my mind more at ease. I was still the number one guy.

Things went on as normal from there. I thought about the Toronado from time to time and sighed over its loss, but I was too busy to really dwell on the strange occurrence of its disappearance. It was gone, and that was sad, but I had a million other things to do.

And then, one day, the dealership's owner called me into his office.

"Steve," he said as I walked by his door. "Come in, come in."

I stopped short and turned to go in slowly, sure that something bad was about to go down; the guy hadn't talked to me like that—all friendly, so fake—in weeks. Not since the Toronado had disappeared. Though he hadn't come right out and said it, I knew that he suspected I'd had something (or maybe everything) to do with the theft. For once in my life, I was innocent. The whole situation made me sick to my stomach, but there was nothing I could do about it.

And when I walked into the office, that feeling just got worse. Standing off to the right was a uniformed cop who did not seem fazed at all by the way I jumped when I saw him.

My mind was racing. Was the cop there for me? He must have been—why else would the boss call me in while he was there? Did the cop know what I was up to? About my drug sales, and my wise guy friends? Was he there to pick me up for any number of crimes I'd never been busted for? Or—oh no, did he find out about the money I'd been—

"Steve," the owner said. "This officer is from the Newark Police Department's stolen car unit. He came to inform me that your car was recovered." He stood behind his desk, arms folded across his chest like a school principal who was very disappointed in my behavior, very disappointed indeed.

"Oh yeah?" I said, trying not to sound too excited or too interested; I knew he still didn't entirely believe that I had nothing to do with the car's disappearance, and I'd been very carefully monitoring my reactions to anything he said about it. "Where?"

The cop stepped toward me, and I instinctively recoiled. He held his arm out, trying to hand me something. "Take it," he said rather calmly, and so I did.

Turning it over in my hands, I found that he'd given me a Polaroid picture with "Property of Newark PD" scribbled in black marker across the bottom. The photo showed my Toronado, doors open, with no tires and no seats. It no longer gleamed; in fact, it looked like it had spent a few years underwater. *Oh, my car,* I lamented silently, my eyes riveted to the photograph, memorizing the image of my former demo, now ripped to shreds and parked right in front of—

Oh, shit. I looked up at my boss, and he was smirking. "Is this some kind of joke?" I asked.

"Afraid not," said the police officer, snatching his photo back and stuffing it into his shirt pocket. "The Oldsmobile was found parked outside that residence early this morning."

"That's my fucking house!" I shouted. "In Newark! That's where I grew up. Jesus Christ, what's my car doing there!"

"Sir, we have already determined that the house was your former place of residence," the officer went on. "We ran your name through the system—"

"You *what*? What for? Am I a suspect or something? You've got to be kidding—"

"Just a routine," the cop said, holding his hands up in front of him, obviously enjoying this opportunity to play peacemaker.

"Yeah, I'll bet," I said, then turned toward the owner, ready to give him a big, fat piece of my mind over all this. I found him glaring at me, eyebrows raised.

"Anything you want to tell me about this situation?" the officer interrupted me.

"Yeah," I said. "Why don't you find the guys who stole my car!" I turned on my heel and went back into the showroom and then straight to my parts department, where I hid in my office for the rest of the day, worrying that the police were going to come back and arrest me at any moment. It was a familiar feeling that came to me easily; living with the threat of incarceration, it seemed, was just like riding a bicycle. I may have fallen off for a while, but once I was back on the seat, feet pedaling furiously, I knew that I had only one way to go.

Chapter 22

Suddenly, I was the focus of an investigation, and everyone seemed to know it. The other managers I'd been friends with—the ones I'd always gone on those long lunches with—could barely look me in the eye anymore, and my own employees seemed to be almost scared of me. Everyone sat on eggshells when I was in the room. I became paranoid, thinking that these people should be worshiping me, not avoiding me. None of it, in my mind, made any sense.

The owner, the boss, the one who'd started all the problems for me this time around, did not seem like he was about to back down, no matter what I did. I argued with him, I pleaded with him, I explained again and again that I had nothing to do with stealing the car, but he didn't want to hear any of it. Finally, after a few too many days of sitting in my office and pondering just how I would end his life if given the chance, when he came in for a "quick word" about the inventory that was coming up at the dealership, I just completely lost it on him. I told him where he could stick his inventory, and exactly what sort of a piece of shit I thought he was.

I pulled the keys to my new demo car from my suit jacket's pocket and threw them at him; he flinched satisfyingly as they hit his chest and clattered to the floor. Feeling that my work there was done, I simply walked out of the dealership, went home, and stayed there. My days of making money for that bastard were over. I was never going back.

By that time, I hadn't had a day off in years, and I had no idea what to do with myself once I got home. I got high, I drank, I watched TV, I called some people, and mostly, I was just plain bored. I didn't know how to relax; I didn't understand the concept of time off. I had to be working, moving, *doing* at all times or everything, it seemed, would come crashing down around me.

To combat this confusion—and to keep my mind off the fact that my work files, the ones that detailed all my fiscal wrongdoings, were completely unguarded at my former office—I tried to stay as high as possible for as long as possible. A couple of days after I walked out of the dealership, I was sitting at my kitchen table doing cocaine, unsure of what time it was or even what day; I felt like I hadn't moved from that chair in a week, but had just been sitting there, snorting and drinking and avoiding anything resembling real life.

The phone rang, and I stumbled up out of my chair and answered it with a slurred greeting. It was one of the managers from Cadillac—one who'd dropped me like a hot potato when the whole Toronado debacle had begun. "What the fuck you want?" I asked him, trying to sound as mean as possible, hoping that he was really fearing for his life on the other end of the phone line.

"Steve, listen to me," he said quietly, as though trying to not be heard by anyone else. "They've been doing the inventory here and shit is missing, man. They're coming over there now to talk to you about it."

"Who?" I asked drunkenly. "Who's coming here? I'll kick their—"

"Steve!" he said, and I could tell that his teeth were clenched; he really was trying to keep this phone call a secret, but he was losing patience with me fast. "The *police* are *on* their *way*. Do you understand what I'm telling you? Whatever you have there, you need to get rid of it. Right. Now."

I stared off into space for a moment, my jaw gone slack, my mind working up to a coherent thought on this new turn of events. *Police*, I thought. *Here. Now.*

"Shit!" I yelled, slamming the phone down. I pulled a box of big, black trash bags out of a kitchen cabinet and opened one up, then went to the bedroom and started tossing stuff into it: the pistol I had under the mattress, the sawed-off shotgun from the closet, the cocaine, my scales, scraps of paper with random phone numbers on them, anything I could see that might implicate me in some sort of illegal activity. When I had that all packed up, I grabbed my keys and headed outside, to my storage shed to get the rest.

Every tenant in the building had a shed like mine, to store stuff they couldn't fit in their apartments, like bicycles and lawn chairs and boxes of old tax returns. You know, normal detritus that normal people had. In my shed, though? That wasn't quite the case.

I popped open the padlock on the door and slid it open. After a quick survey of the contents within, I billowed open a new black plastic bag and started loading stuff into it—blocks of cocaine, bags of pills, mostly. With a quick look behind me to make sure that no nosy neighbors were peeking out at me from behind their curtains, I slung the full bag over my shoulder, like some twisted Santa Claus, and headed toward my other secret stash: my second shed.

I'd acquired this supplemental storage area from the building's landlord, whom I partied with from time to time. A while back, in exchange for some really good blow, he'd given me access to this secret shed to store contraband in, just for occasions such as the one I was in the middle of. I hadn't used it yet, up until then, but as I slipped my key into its industrial-strength lock, I was heartily grateful for it. I tossed my sack of incriminating evidence inside, locked it up again, and got away from it as quickly as possible.

When the cops arrived, I was sitting on my sofa, watching television and enjoying a nice vodka and tonic. I was polite to them, even urbane, chit-chatting and offering them some refreshing beverages of their own—ha ha, just joking, officers! No vodka for you while you're on the clock, protecting the world from bad guys like me! They didn't seem entirely impressed with my Mr. Innocent act, but they didn't throw me up against the wall and strip-search me, either, so I figured that things were going pretty well. In all, they searched my apartment for two hours, and they found nothing. As far as they knew, I was as squeaky clean as they were, and if it hadn't been for the little problem of the thousands of dollars that they already knew I'd stolen from my place of employment, they really would have had a hard time pinning anything on me at all.

Chapter 23

"Get me the fuck out of here!" I yelled at Donna through the thick glass partition of the Clifton jail's visiting room. "I don't want to say here another minute, do you hear me?"

She sighed wearily but smiled, trying as always to placate me. "I'll get you out just as soon as I possibly can, Steve. You know, your bail is twenty-five thousand, but you only need ten percent to get out... I sold some of my jewelry today and I think I have enough."

"Good," I said offhandedly. "Now just get me the fuck out of here."

I really should have been more grateful for what Donna was doing for me. I had no money to my name, nothing put aside in case of emergency; as always, even with the money I'd stolen, I'd spent everything as soon as I'd had it in my hand. I'd never thought about the future. Savings accounts and retirement plans? Not exactly top priorities for a guy like me.

But my lack of assets didn't stop me from continuing to think that I was better than every single person who had made it their business to put me in jail that day. The Cadillac dealership owner, the people who did the inventory, the cops who arrested me, the guards, the judge—all assholes. After Donna left and I had nothing to do but sit in my cell and stare at the wall, I passed time by imagining the ways in which I would make each of them pay when and if they crossed my path again.

Donna sprung me later that day and I went back to my apartment in Nutley, where I holed myself up like a lab rat in a cage. I paced the floor, chain-smoking and drinking straight from the vodka bottle, trying to figure out what to do with my life from then on. I didn't have a job anymore, and since everyone at Cadillac knew what I'd done—and that I'd been arrested for it—there was no way I'd get work in the same industry ever again. I resigned myself, then and there, to not even look for a new job. Why should I bother, if it was only going to end in defeat?

In the days and weeks to follow, my rent came due and went unpaid; so did every other bill I had in my name. I had no money coming in, no car to drive, no food in my refrigerator. Donna visited and gave me what she could financially, but she wasn't loaded, either, and even her generosity had its limits. When it came down to it, I was alone and broke, and just out of luck in general.

But as usual, when I had not a thing to my name, I could always find some way to get what I needed, and what I needed at that time was pills. Not cocaine, not heroin—pills. My standby. My old friends, who had gotten me through so many rough times before. I wanted them, and I wanted them bad.

I'd been using pills all along, even through my adventures in cocaine land, though by that time they were called "hits" and I no longer needed the codeine-laced cough medicine to go with them. The old sleeping pills of my younger days had evolved, and now it all came together in one handy little tablet. Advances in modern medicine certainly were a wonderful thing, and I reaped their benefits on a daily basis.

I had a regular dealer whom I bought my hits from, and I invited him over to the Passion Pit to hook me up. When he got there and I told him that I was flat out of cash, he didn't seem too disturbed. We'd come up with some pretty good arrangements in the past when I'd been short on funds, and I was confident that we could work something out this time, too. An hour later, when he was leaving with some of my appliances and most of my furniture, and I had a bag full of pills in my hand, I was satisfied that we'd made a pretty good deal.

After that, I spent days sitting on the floor in the nearly bare apartment, taking pills, smoking cigarettes and nodding out. And just like that, all my troubles seemed to disappear. I was back to normal; I'd returned to my level of comfort. Everything, for me, was just as it was supposed to be.

After a while, when I realized that I was running out of hits, I tried to go back to my mobster friends to get a job, but they no longer seemed to need me—I couldn't fix their cars for free anymore, and on top of that I had legal problems, so I was of no use to them whatsoever. I was more like a plague they wanted to avoid; they barely even wanted to look at me, much less let me handle their money. At that point, I was someone dangerous to them, someone who could get them into a lot of trouble. For once, I was a badder dude than they were. I guessed that I'd finally gotten what I'd wanted.

Chapter 24

With old habits came old problems, and before long I found myself arrested for possession of narcotics, and just like in the old days, I was dragged down to the Essex County Jail. I was given a ninety-day sentence and thrown into a dank cell, which at least was private. I even had a quiet neighbor—a real blessing in any lockup situation.

After a few days, I became curious about this guy in the next cell. He didn't shout or talk to himself, or exhibit any of the other signs of life that I heard constantly from the other inmates around me. One night I asked a guard what was up with the guy, and I found out that he was asleep most of the time because of some medication they had him on, and of course, I was immediately jealous. I wished I had something to knock me out and make the whole nightmare go away.

Another day, I caught my neighbor awake; I could hear him shuffling around his cell. I called over and said hello, and introduced myself, and he seemed friendly enough, though everything he said was punctuated by a lot of yawning. Though I'd heard his supposed story from the guard already, I wanted to verify that it was true, so I asked him why he was like that—why he was practically comatose most of the time. "You've gotta be getting something good from these jerks," I told him. "Am I right?"

Turned out, I *was* right—he said that he was getting pills for some condition he had. I don't remember now what it was, and back then, I really I didn't care. All I heard was the word "pills," and my mind started churning. I didn't know what he was taking, but I knew that I wanted some of it for myself.

So I made him a deal: If he gave me his next dose of whatever he was on, I'd give him a bunch of cigarettes, which I bought with the money Donna regularly deposited into my jail bank account. I was grateful to her for that—couldn't live without my smokes— and now that I knew that I could trade them for something even better, well, I was thanking her even more.

My neighbor agreed to the trade, and the next time his pills came around, he handed one over to me. I lay down on my cot, slipped the pill into my mouth and swallowed it slowly, like it was a delicacy that I wanted to savor. I tried to psych myself into believing that the medication was really doing something to me. My head started to swim like it did when I got high, and a smile spread across my face as I anticipated the sweet, sleepy feeling that would surely follow.

But then, something went seriously, *seriously* wrong. Instead of relaxing, my entire body stiffened up, and I couldn't move. I yelled out to a guard—screamed for him like I was being murdered— who in turn called an ambulance and had me rushed to the emergency room at St. Michael's in Newark. I was in really horrible shape—all my joints were locked up, my muscles almost paralyzed. In the ER, they gave me a shot that loosened me up again. I found out later that while the guy from the next cell had given me his Thorazine, he hadn't given me the muscle relaxant that was supposed to go with it. Greedy bastard had to keep that for himself, and by doing that, he almost killed me.

When they brought me back to jail, I expected to have the book thrown at me. Taking another inmate's medication? Bribing him for it with cigarettes? Going to the hospital on the legal system's dime? All offenses that I knew could get a hefty amount of time added on to my sentence. But as the days went on—each one spent peering out my cell door, waiting to see a public defender coming in to tell me my fate—I started to think that nothing was going to happen. Once, a guard made me submit a urine specimen for drug testing, but I never even got a report of what the results were. Just like it was out on the streets of Newark, it seemed like there were bigger things going on out in the general population, and no one worried much about a small-time pill popper like me.

Donna came to visit me in jail from time to time, and seeing her pretty face was always a relief. Being the asshole that I was, I never really questioned why she spent so much time, energy and money on such a loser, but other people certainly did; once, when she was leaving the visitation room, I heard a guard asking her why she was wasting her time on me. When I tried to get in his face about it, he just towered over me and said, "You should kiss the ground she walks on." I backed off, only partially admitting, and only in the back of my mind, that he was right.

In all, I did seventy-five of the ninety days I was supposed to serve in the Essex County Jail, and then I was released for good behavior or some ridiculous thing like that. Donna came to pick me up and brought me to a hotel room she'd rented for me, since I'd lost my apartment while I was locked up. She had a bottle of champagne chilling on the dresser, like it was some sort of celebration, and as we drank up, she told me how much she wanted to help me get back on track, like I'd ever been on any kind of track to begin with.

The next day, she bought me a beat-up old car for five hundred dollars and got me a place to live in Kearny; she would pay the rent—a hundred dollars a week—until I got back on my feet. She also helped me apply for a few jobs—menial stuff, work that I thought was below me, even given the sorry state I was in. A muffler shop in Newark was stupid enough to hire me, and I re-entered the world of gainful employment with little enthusiasm. I was back to being a nothing, a nobody, one working stiff among a million, and I certainly, definitely didn't like it.

When I got my first paycheck, tiny though it was compared to what I used to earn at Cadillac, I went out and spent it all on hits. By that time, I was totally addicted to the pills again; I needed them, had no choice, just had to have them. If I tried to skip even one day, it was horrible for me physically, and I did not want to end up in the hospital again.

When I had no money of my own, I got some off Donna, claiming that I needed groceries or just a little more to pay a bill, and she never questioned me on it. When I didn't feel like I could ask her for any more, I at least always knew that she'd be giving me money for rent once a month, and I could use a little of that to get what I needed. Eventually, I just didn't pay the rent anymore; it all went to buy hits. And when that source of funds ran out, I traded the car she'd bought me for dope.

Like I said, I was an asshole. But what I was doing was nothing compared to things that were yet to come.

Chapter 25

"Vinny," I said into the phone, quietly as I could. "You gotta get me outta here. You don't know what it's like."

I heard my oldest brother sigh, that long-suffering sound that I'd heard from so many people in my life by that time. "No, I don't know what it's like," he said. "I—"

"They're *beating* me *up* here, Vinny!" I said desperately. "*Beating* me. Every fucking day. It's like—"

"Being in jail?" I thought I heard him snickering.

"Funny. Now will you please come down here with some money and bail me out?"

Another sigh. "Fine," he said. "Tomorrow. I'll be there tomorrow."

I hung up the pay phone and told the guard I was ready to go back to the group holding cell I'd been in since that morning. When I then informed him that in twenty-four hours, I would be out of that shit-hole, he shoved me from behind and told me to keep walking.

Nelson Place in downtown Newark wasn't the best jail in town, but it definitely wasn't the worst, either. It was overcrowded, full of jerks, smelly—all the things a lockup was supposed to be. Whenever I was there, I had to share a cell with twenty other deadbeats who were waiting to be processed, and the guards left a lot to be desired when it came to tender loving care.

But, despite what I'd told my brother, no one had actually hit me. In fact, aside from that little push I'd just received, barely anyone touched me on purpose. That was just something I'd made up so that Vinny would think I was in some real danger; I'd have told him anything I could to make him feel sorry for me, anything that would get him to come down and bail me out.

Back in the cell, I announced my good news to some of the inmates I'd been hanging around with—Italians like myself, fellow wannabe mobsters I'd come to make friends with during my short stay.

"Steve," one of them said to me conspiratorially, taking a wad of bills out of his pants pockets, throwing a look toward the guards outside as he did so. Cash was forbidden in jail—you'd get another charge pinned on you if you were caught with any sort of money on your person.

"When you get out," this guy whispered to me, "put this money in my account for me. I'm gonna borrow some cigarettes today, and I'll be able to pay them back tomorrow if you can do me this favor."

Cigarettes were the great currency in jail—you smoked them, you loaned them, you traded them for other goods. An inmate was only as good as the number of packs he owned, and the only way to get said packs was to have money in your spending account at the jail, so you could buy them from the jail itself.

"Yeah, me too!" another chimed in, pulling out his own stack of bills. "I've been waiting to find someone I can trust with all this cash I got. I can trust you, right?"

"Sure," I answered. I collected the money from those two and a couple others, promising them that as soon as I was released, I would put what they gave me into their accounts.

The next day, Vinny came and bailed me out. Once outside, I shook his hand and thanked him—especially when he gave me an additional few bucks to get a hotel room. I had no place to stay, and I guess he had a little pity for me after all.

Once Vinny left, and I was alone on the streets once again, I took off down the block, in search of my dealer. I needed pills, and I had a whole lot of other people's money burning a hole in my pocket.

Three weeks later, I was arrested again and put back in the Essex County Jail at Nelson Place. The disgustingly dirty mattress on the floor of the holding cell had barely gone cold before I was slumped over on it once again, giving my back to everyone else who was penned up in there with me, trying to get my mind off the fact that I was going to be without pills for quite a while. I was sick and going through withdrawal already, and I just wanted to sleep.

And I might have been successful in this endeavor if it hadn't been for the son of a bitch who thought it would be funny to toss a wet roll of toilet paper at my head. I knew what it was as soon as it hit me; I also knew that I was in for some trouble. If there was any doubt, the second roll that hit me made it very clear.

I sat up on the mattress, reached for my nearby shoes and put them on slowly; I knew that whichever scumbag was trying to start something with me was itchy to get it on already, and rule number one, I had to have my shoes on if I was going to get into a fight. When I was finally ready, I stood up and said, "Come on, let's get it over with. I'm tired of this bullshit and I'm not feeling good."

And then, I turned around and got a good look at the culprit. *Oh, shit*, I thought. It was one of the Italian guys whose money I'd ripped off the last time, and he had five or six Spanish friends with him. They walked toward me across the cell, and the rest of the crowd parted like... Well, like a bunch of people getting the hell out of the way because they knew there was about to be a big fight.

But before this little gang reached me, it stopped, and the Italian guy peered behind me. I flicked my head around as fast as I could—rule number two, never take your eyes off someone who wants to kill you—and found that I had my own posse backing me up: a black guy, huge and full of muscles, whom I had gone to grade school with, and a couple of his equally meaty friends.

Turning back to the Italian, I saw him snap back and try to recover, trying to keep his composure. "Is there a problem?" he asked the guys behind me, trying to sound like the mobster he thought he was.

"There's no problem," my old friend said sedately. "Just making things even."

I stood there and looked at the Italian guy. I was ready for a fair fight with him, but he backed off. It was over, and everyone knew it. He'd been humiliated, and I hadn't even had to lift a finger. Best of all, because of this incident, I got moved to another floor of the jail, where I didn't have to deal with assholes like him anymore.

Chapter 26

When I wasn't in jail, all I did was walk the streets of Newark day and night, always high. I had no home, no possessions, no friends and no family who wanted me, though I couldn't blame any of them for that; Donna came looking for me from time to time and tried to help me out, but mostly I just took her money and went on with my life. She was a good woman, a smart woman. She could have done so much better for herself if she'd just left me alone.

Having nowhere to sleep meant I had nowhere to bathe, and I grew dirtier and dirtier every day. The worse I looked, it seemed, the less I cared, and I slowly turned into the sort of guy I thought I'd never become: one who didn't even notice how bad he smelled, who picked up used cigarette butts from the ground and smoked them, who talked to himself because there was no one else around who wanted to listen.

Though I didn't consider myself homeless or anything, that's essentially what I was, and I found that people treated me as such: either looking away so they didn't have to see me, or looking down on me with distaste, or, for the very few, showing me kindness that I never would have expected. One day, while I nodded off against the side of a building, a woman came up and wrapped a blanket around me. If I'd been a few degrees further toward lucidity, I might have thanked her.

When the weather was bad, or when I'd just had enough of sleeping on sidewalks, I found shelter wherever I could. I had a mental list of abandoned buildings where I could take cover when need be, to sleep off whatever I was on with a hundred other junkies.

One morning, I was walking out of one of these places—a particularly dank former warehouse, where I'd just spent a long night, huddled under the blanket that woman had given me and just waiting for the sun to come up. There were cops stationed in a cruiser outside—not looking to bust anyone, I guessed, but just following their regular beat. As I walked by, one of them stuck his head out the open car window and said, "Hey, did you just come out of that heartbreak hotel?" I've never forgotten that phrase. Just hearing it made me feel awful.

I had an uncle—the one who'd brought me to the hospital on Christmas Eve way back, when I'd turned myself into a living statue—who owned an insurance agency in Belleville, not too far from Newark. I remembered him one day, kind of out of the blue, and the thought of him stuck in my mind for a while. I'd always liked this uncle. He'd always been pretty nice to me, even when I probably hadn't deserved it.

So one day, I got up the nerve to go and visit him—honestly, to see if he would give me some money that I could get high with. I made my way to his office and walked in, and he was sitting there at his desk. He just looked at me for a minute or two, and then got up, came over and gave me a hug.

"Where's your other shoe?" he asked, and I looked down at my feet—only one of them was covered. I wondered how long I'd been ambling around with a naked foot. I just looked at my uncle and shrugged.

He ushered me into the back room and sat me down, commenting that I didn't have a coat, either, and that I should have one—it was getting colder by the day outside and I should take better care of myself. He busied himself with this mindless chatter while he gave me something to eat, maybe the lunch he'd brought for himself that day. I don't remember what it was, but I practically inhaled it, not because I liked it but because I wanted to get it over with. The only thing I was concerned with was getting money to get pills, and letting him fuss over me seemed like the only route to that destination.

Before I left, I had new shoes on my feet and a coat on my back, but no money; my uncle wouldn't give me any, and I really couldn't blame him. As we said goodbye, he had tears in his eyes, and if I had been able to cry myself, I probably would have, too. I patted him on the shoulder and thanked him for his kindness, then walked out the door.

Making my way slowly back down the sidewalk, I thought about what I'd just done, and after a couple of blocks, I realized just how awful I was. Using my uncle like that? Going to see him, just to get money, when I hadn't even made an effort to call him in years? What an asshole I was. I'd tried to use him like I'd used everyone else.

Ambling down the cold road, I didn't know who I should feel worse for: my uncle or myself. The more I thought about it, the slower my gait became, weighed down by the enormous load of embarrassment I dragged behind me like a big, dead thing tied to my legs. I wished that I could just end my life.

Chapter 27

Winter came full on, and I was still living on the streets. Every day, the weather got worse; every night, I was sure that I would freeze to death in whatever rat trap I'd managed to find to sleep in.

One day, during my roaming—that's all I did was walk around, trying to get money, looking for pills and a place to sleep—I came across an open window on the back of an apartment building. I'd never been in there before, which meant that probably, nobody else had, either, which meant that I might have found myself a little privacy for once. I pushed the window in, and it swung open; it was just big enough for me to squeeze through. Once inside, I landed on the floor with a thud and found myself in a basement. A boiler room, to be exact. The place was so warm, I had to take my coat off.

Night was coming on, and I was ready for a good nap, so I found myself a dark corner and curled up on the floor. It wasn't clean, and it wasn't soft, but the place was quiet and for the first time in a long time, I didn't have to wonder too much if I'd be alive in the morning.

And my first assessment had been right, it seemed: None of the other vagrants in the area knew about this building, because for that night, and every one after it for quite a while, I had the boiler room all to myself. After a week or so of breathing in the fumes from the ancient, rumbling heating machine, I had black rings around my nose, and I could only imagine what it was making my lungs look like—though with the amount I smoked, it probably didn't make any difference.

During the day, I left this secret enclave of mine and went to work, stealing and selling, to get money to get high. Pills were my one motivation in life, the only thing that kept me going from day to day.

I spent Christmas Eve 1983 in this boiler room, lying on the floor in the dark, staring up at the ceiling. I could see through its cracks, through the floorboards and up into the apartment above my hideout. I'd been watching the family there off and on for a while, whenever I could steal a glimpse of them. They seemed like nice people, though I imagined that if they knew I was sleeping in their basement every night, they wouldn't be so happy.

They had a small Christmas tree up there—I could see the glow of its lights, and I spaced out for a while just staring at them. The family was having a dinner that smelled really good, and I could hear them talking and laughing. They probably had presents to open later on, and I'd silently witness that too, without their knowledge.

I thought about Christmases with my family, when I was a kid, before Mom had gotten sick, and the few holidays I'd gotten to spend with my own young daughters. I couldn't even remember the last time I'd seen them, much less the last Christmas gifts I'd given them. As I listened to the family upstairs saying grace before their meal, I felt more alone than I ever had in my life, and that was saying a lot.

Because I was doing so much criminal stuff—stealing, selling, possession of narcotics, breaking and entering—the frequency of my arrests doubled, or maybe tripled. Whatever it was, it was a lot. I was always either in jail, trying to get out of jail or worrying about going back to jail.

I wasn't always arrested when I was high, but I was always high when I was arrested; there's no doubt that my drug use contributed to my own personal rate of incarceration. Actually, really, drugs were about the *only* reason why I ever did the illegal things I did—I may have been a criminal, but I wasn't *evil*. I didn't *enjoy* stealing, and I surely didn't just do it for the hell of it. Every bad thing I ever did was because of drugs and alcohol. I'm not saying that it's a good excuse; it's just a fact of my life.

Most of the time, when I was arrested in those days, I was first brought to the jail at Green Street. This place was the biggest hellhole in the city, which is saying a lot. There were an awful lot of nasty places in Newark, and Green Street topped them all.

To start with, it smelled like a locker room—like there was a secret stash of old gym socks hidden somewhere inside it, just festering and stinking the whole place up. On top of that, it was always freezing cold, and the all-concrete-and-cement décor didn't help with that any. The guards were basically sadistic jerks who didn't even let the prisoners shower for days or weeks at a time.

Basically, you wouldn't find anything even in the worst horror movie that could compare to Green Street in its heyday. It was terrible, inhumane, the kind of place Geraldo Rivera liked to do exposés about. Much later, it was actually closed down because it was such a dungeon, and I'm sure that no one was sorry to see it go.

Now my brother Nicky, the cop, worked at that time in the Newark Police Department's headquarters—which were located directly above the Green Street jail. It was a perfect place for him because *like* him, it had absolutely no give whatsoever. Nicky had no gray areas, and neither did Green Street; they were both strict, severe and, on the whole, unforgiving. Sometimes, I wondered if he'd requested to have his office right over the jail, because the match was so goddamn perfect.

Whenever I was in a cell at Green Street, I spent my time lying on a cot, staring at the ceiling, knowing that my brother was working in the precinct upstairs. He never came down to see me, to ask how I was doing, to see if he could help me out at all. Now, of course, I don't blame him at all for that; I might have even acted the same way, had the shoe been on the other foot. I can only imagine the shame he must have felt—a cop with his younger brother locked up right downstairs.

Chapter 28

Anyone who was arrested downtown was sent to Green Street because it was like a holding tank for the Essex County Jail. You got picked up, you got thrown in a cell, you got your five minutes in court and then they shipped you off to the big house, more likely than not. It was a process that, before long, I'd become very familiar with.

Once, when I was locked up there, my time came up and the guards pulled me out of my cell and led me to the court, where I'd hear all about what I'd done—damned if I could remember it myself. I was dazed, dirty and cold, miserable and actually wishing that they'd let me go back to the cell so I could lie down.

As I shuffled along, just one in a group of inmates who were all en route to appear before the judge, a black guy next to me leaned over and whispered, "You know how to get out of here, don't you?"

I looked at him slowly, my eyes half closed. I felt so weak, just exhausted and hungry and ready to give up. I didn't feel like making friendly conversation, but despite my lack of response, the guy went on.

"How long you been down here?" he asked me. "Since you had a shower or ate right? Don't you want to get out of here?"

"Yes," I answered without even looking at him.

"Then when the judge asks you a question," the guy continued, "tell him to go fuck himself. Just like that: 'Go fuck yourself, your honor.' You do that, and they'll take you right out to the county jail. It's so much better there."

He was right—things were better at the county jail. There was heat, at least, and food, and guards who let you bathe. I had a vision of it in my mind like it was some sort of paradise; I could almost smell the soap. Figuring that I had nothing left to lose—I was already in jail—I nodded at my new friend and kept on walking toward the courtroom.

When my turn came in front of the judge, I stood there with my head down, not because I was ashamed of myself but because I was tired and sick. I heard my charges read but barely comprehended them, and when the judge asked me how I pled, I mumbled out just what that guy had told me to: "Your honor, go fuck yourself."

"Excuse me?" the judge asked, unable to hear me—my head hanging down as it was, I was pretty much talking into my shirt.

I raised my head up high, closed my eyes and took a deep breath. Then, with all the force I could muster, I opened my mouth and repeated, "GO. FUCK. YOURSELF. SIR."

He banged his gavel so hard it nearly broke in half. "Thirty days' confinement!" he yelled.

"Go fuck yourself!" I told him again.

Well, that did it. The guards manhandled me out of the room, and I knew that soon, I'd be on my way to sixty days of incarcerated bliss.

Other times at Green Street, though, things didn't go quite so well. Once, I was put into a cell with a gunshot victim who had pins going through his arm; it was a disgusting, messy sight and if I hadn't been so high, I might not have been able to look at it for as long as I did. Someone at the jail had given him a bottle of peroxide to clean his wounds once an hour, and I watched him out of morbid interest and lack of anything else to do.

When this guy went to sleep, he left his bottle of peroxide next to his bed. I sat there on the floor—there was only one cot in the cell, and you had to be pretty big, or pretty injured, to get it—wide-eyed, staring and staring at the stuff, wondering what it would do to my insides if I drank it. Had to be something bad, I was sure, and that idea excited and comforted me at the same time. *I could end it all*, I thought, squinting at the bottle in the darkness.

Before I could stop myself, I leaned over, picked up the bottle, popped off the cap and put it to my lips. Intending to down the whole thing, I leaned my head back and took a swig, welcoming the drama of killing myself by antiseptic ingestion.

But as soon as the liquid hit my tongue, I knew that it had been a bad, *bad* idea. The taste—oh, God, it was beyond awful. It burned my mouth and throat, and made tears spring to my eyes. I spit it out in a spray all over my cellmate and coughed like I was about to vomit up my intestines.

When I started yelling for help, a couple of guards ran over— well, walked over a little faster than usual; they didn't run for anything around there, and certainly not unless they were summoned. "Holy shit," one of them said to the other, stopping outside the bars and pointing at me. "He drank the fucking peroxide. He's foaming at the mouth!"

I put my fingers up to my lips and indeed, I was foaming, which kind of made me start screaming. I knew, logically, that it was just from the peroxide—you put it on your skin, it gets sudsy, that's the magic of it—but feeling it running out of my mouth like that was just too much.

I was still holding the bottle in my hand, but as the guards unlocked the cell door and came in to collect me, I dropped it on the floor, letting whatever was left run out onto the concrete. I looked over at the gunshot guy as the guards grabbed my arms and complained about having to take me to the hospital. He'd slept through the whole thing.

At the hospital, they basically laughed at me and gave me some stuff to flush out my system, in case any of the peroxide had made its way into my stomach. Lying there in the bed—which, at least, was more comfortable than what I had at Green Street—I accepted the fact that I didn't have the guts to kill myself. In all honesty, I was kind of disappointed.

Chapter 29

When I was sent back to the jail, I decided I'd have enough of the place, and I resorted to my last of all resorts: calling Vinny and asking him to bail me out again. I wasn't hopeful that it would work, but with no other choices, at least I had to try.

At Green Street, there was one phone that all the prisoners used, and it was passed down from cell to cell, so if you were at the end of the line and itching to get out, you were shit out of luck. Every call from that phone had to be collect, and when I called my brother, his wife answered, and she accepted the reversed charges. *One hurdle down*, I told myself, thankful that she had at least been willing to talk to me.

Before she had a chance to say anything, I started in on how bad it was in the jail—and this time, I wasn't lying. After outlining a few of the more horrific aspects of my confinement, I put all my self-respect aside and asked her if she could help me get out.

Now, I knew it wasn't going to be an easy phone call; I wasn't even really expecting her and Vinny to help me. But what I certainly wasn't expecting was a Sunday school class. My sister-in-law launched into such a speech about the Lord, how he would help me get through my troubles and how I shouldn't worry—all that "this too shall pass" stuff. She meant well, even then I knew that she did, but I just couldn't take it. No matter what response I gave her, from a grunt to a frustrated "yeah, yeah, got it," she just kept on going, getting out what she wanted to say, whether I wanted to hear it or not.

"Don't worry," she told me finally. "You're strong. You're a good kid, other than the drugs. You'll get through it. You take care now, Steve. Bye bye."

I hung up the phone and passed it on to the outstretched hands at the next cell, wondering, as I went back to bed, what the fuck I'd called for. She wasn't going to help me. Vinny wasn't going to help me. Nicky wasn't going to help me, even though he was one goddamn floor up from where I was being held. If my own family had given up on me, then God must've too, and my sister-in-law was wrong. No one was going to take care of me but me, and that was just something I was going to have to get used to.

I was lying on the floor of my cell, pondering this new development, thinking that I'd never get out of there, when I heard a cop yelling, "Della Valle!" I jumped up as the cell door opened and a guard informed me that Donna had come down, without telling me, to bail me out. She'd also left me ten dollars to get something to eat.

As I walked down the street, away from the jailhouse, I thought about some of the things I used to like to eat: hot dogs, sub sandwiches, all the things I'd missed while I was incarcerated. And then, I made an abrupt turn into the first liquor store I saw and bought a bottle of Majorska vodka with the money Donna had left me. I started drinking it before I even got my change.

Later that night, I was rearrested for burglary and thrown back in the very same cell at Green Street. The guy I'd been with earlier was still there, still sleeping. He didn't even know that I'd been gone.

Early one morning, some time after being let out of jail again, I was walking around Newark, as usual. I had a few dollars in my pocket—enough to buy some pills, enough to keep me high for most of the day. Normally, this would be a good thing.

That day, though, something was not right in my head. I didn't know why, but I just did not want to get high. I didn't feel like it, couldn't wrap my brain around it. I just wanted to try to get through a day without doing anything, maybe to prove to myself that I could do so without being incarcerated.

Was I thinking that I should stop altogether? I don't know. I did consider that once in a while, but never seriously. It takes a lot of effort, a lot of determination to kick a drug habit and most of the time, in those days, I lacked that particular brand of will power. I knew that I could do it again if I got back on methadone, but again, to do that, I would actually have to put forth some conscious effort.

I thought about methadone sometimes, and reminisced about my days at the clinic. I knew that I was looking back on them through some rosy lenses—anything compared to my current situation had to look pretty good—but I really believed that my life had been just a little bit better back then. I'd been clean, I'd had a job, and I'd met my wife, for whatever that was worth. I tended to use that period as a yardstick of sorts, to measure the rest of my life against. Nothing ever came close, though, which just made me more depressed, and pushed me further into a world of reclusive addiction.

But that morning, that one strange morning when I woke up feeling like I wanted to be clean for a day, was like a breath of long-awaited fresh air. I felt good about the decision, renewed somehow. I strolled down the street with my head up a little higher than usual, my back a little straighter. There was even a little bit of spring in my step. I felt like I should be celebrating.

Yes… Celebrating, I thought slowly, a smile creeping across my face. *Why not? This is some momentous occasion.*

With that idea in mind, I stepped into a local bodega and headed to the back of the store, toward the refrigerator cases, to check out their alcoholic offerings. A celebration called for a drink, I figured, just a little nip to toast myself and the excellent choice I had made.

Though I usually drank the hard stuff, I saw something new in the bodega that day—they were called wine coolers, and I had no idea what they were. They looked good, though, so I bought one, and drank it right there in front of the counter.

"Man," I said after I'd downed the whole thing in one shot. "That's tasty."

It was so good, in fact, that I bought another, and another, and before I knew it I'd had—well, I don't know how many. But it was a lot, and I was pretty looped by the time I walked out of the store and stumbled back onto the street, all thoughts of staying sober gone, all thoughts of doing the right thing vanished.

Chapter 30

Two hours later, I was in an abandoned building downtown, handing over whatever cash I had left to a dealer. He threw me some pills and I swallowed them immediately, my mind only briefly flickering back to my earlier ruminations about not getting high that day.

Must have been some other person talking, I thought, feeling my muscles sink into the old, familiar relaxation that only my beloved sleeping pills could bring. *I'd never say something as stupid as that.*

And then I was off again, walking up and down the streets of Newark, no particular destination in mind. I ended up, maybe on purpose, in my old neighborhood, where I'd grown up, and from there, made my way to my childhood home: 69 Tiffany Boulevard. I turned the address over and over in my head as I stood in front of the house, trying to call up some sort of memory that would fill me with nostalgia and happiness. Nothing came to mind.

I went around the back of the house and for no reason other than habit—I was always looking for a new place to crash—I tested a few windows to see if any of them were open. Lo and behold, one was—the very window I'd climbed in as a kid, when I hadn't wanted to deal with the family members who would undoubtedly have accosted me if I'd gone in the front door.

Without giving it much thought, I climbed in through this window once more, and found myself in what used to be my bedroom. I stood in the middle of it, dumbly looking around at the walls, which were a different color than what I remembered. Nothing there was familiar anymore, and it made me sad—but at least, I noticed, my bed was still there. Still in the same place and everything. And boy, did I really need a nap.

So, I tumbled down onto the mattress and grabbed at the blankets to cover myself up, letting out a loud sigh as my bleary head hit the pillow. I rolled over, ready to tuck in for a good snooze.

"Good night," I said sleepily to the woman lying next to me.

My eyes popped open. "Oh, shit!"

I leapt out of the bed, and practically right out of my skin, too. I stood there by the side of the bed, holding my hands out to the woman as if to ward off whatever she was planning to do to me. She had the covers pulled up to her chin like some grandma in a fairy tale, and I was the big, bad wolf who had come in to eat her alive.

As I looked around frantically for some clue as to what I should be doing at that point—well, that was when the screaming began.

"Who are you! What are you doing here! Get out! HELP! HEEELLLP!" the woman shrieked—or at least, that's what I guessed she was saying. Her native tongue, apparently, was Spanish, and I actually had no idea what the sounds coming out of her mouth meant at all.

Before I knew what was happening, the bedroom door flew open and a bunch of strapping Puerto Ricans flew in. They grabbed me, hit me, kicked me, and all the while, that woman kept screaming. It was a madhouse, a violent, confusing scene that my doped-up brain was just not able to process.

When my adrenaline finally kicked in, I was able to free myself from the guys, who seemed to want to kill me very badly. I hurled myself back out the window and hit the ground running.

At the front of the house again, I found a woman sitting in an idling car; I pulled open the door, dragged her out onto the pavement and jumped in behind the wheel. I threw the car into drive and just took off as fast as I could.

Halfway down the block, I checked the rearview mirror, and the Spanish guys were coming after me—running down the street in a mob, some holding baseball bats, all looking very pissed off.

"Fuck you!" I yelled, turning around to look at them through the car's back window. "Fuck you!" I gave them the finger. They'd never catch up with me on foot, and just to insult them, I put the gas pedal down to the floor.

When I turned back around to look where I was going, however, my joy came to a very abrupt halt. At the end of the street, there was a police roadblock, of all things. I didn't know if they were looking for me or not, but in a matter of seconds, they were sure going to find me.

I slammed on the brakes and let out a yell as my car plowed into the side of a police cruiser. My whole body was thrown forward and my head hit something, hard—probably the steering wheel. And that was when my entire world went black.

PART TWO

Chapter 31

"What the fuck happened to me?" I repeated, rubbing a hand over my face, trying to get the grogginess out of my head. I shrugged my shoulders and looked back at the public defender I was supposed to know from grade school. "I have no idea. I was hoping you could tell me."

He smiled again, but this time I only glared at him weakly. I was sore, tired, confused, defeated and not in the mood for anything.

"Well, long story short," he said, "you snuck into the house you used to live in, climbed in bed with a woman and got the shit beat out of you by her husband and brothers."

I nodded. Didn't recall a lick of it myself, but his story seemed about right.

"Now, unfortunately," he went on in what sounded like his official lawyer voice, "since I more or less know you, I have to tell the judge that I can't represent you. Another attorney will be assigned to you." He stood up and stuck a hand out for me to shake.

I nodded again. "Understandable," I said, standing up too and gripping his hand loosely.

"Steve," he said seriously, pausing to give me a stern look. "Take care of yourself."

I threw him a half-assed smile, trying not to look too defeated. We said our goodbyes, and he finally let go of my hand. After he walked out of the cell, I lay back down and went straight to sleep. I'd had more than enough bullshit for one day.

Within the week, my new public defender, who didn't know me at all and didn't really make any attempt to do so, got me transferred to Nelson Place while my court date was pending. I was held there on a very high amount of bail that I knew I couldn't even begin to ask anyone to pay for me. I was in it for the long haul at last, and finally, I gave up all hope of ever being a free man again. At last, I just didn't care.

During my indefinite stay at Nelson Place, I was called out to court periodically for other charges that came up against me—possession counts that hadn't been followed through on, no-shows from earlier court dates, whatever they could find. Now that the authorities knew for sure where I was, everything that I'd managed to evade in the past was catching up with me.

The theft charges from the Cadillac dealership came back, too. I didn't know exactly what would happen to me because of them, but I wasn't really worried about it because I had nothing to lose; nothing the legal system could do to me would be worse than anything I'd already done to myself. I had nothing left: no wife, no children, no job, no home, no money… I didn't even have a stinking wallet. A while before, I'd given it to a store owner I'd known as a kid. I'd told him that my car had a dead battery, and he'd given me fifty bucks to fix it; I'd given him my wallet as collateral. I'd taken his money, of course, and never gone back for my wallet.

When I was finally brought to the Passaic County court for the Cadillac charges, it was Halloween, and I felt like a gigantic pumpkin in my bright orange, prison-issued jumpsuit. To make things even more circuslike, the people in charge there weren't very in charge of things at all, and didn't know quite how to get me and the other slobs who had to go to court that day in through the back door. Instead, we were led right up the front steps of the courthouse, weaving our way through all the lawyers and other important-looking people, our shackles clattering as we shuffled on by. I felt all those suit-wearing bozos looking at me with disgust. I bet that they were looking at me and thinking that no matter what their own personal problems were, they could be a whole lot worse.

When the court clerk called my case, I went before the judge and he told me that instead of deciding on my case that day, he'd wait to see what Essex County did with my other charges first. After I was tried and sentenced there, he said, he would decide what else to do with me. A weird verdict, I thought—a sort of nonverdict, really—but I took it for what it was and simply walked out of the courtroom without a word.

When I got back to my cell at the end of the day, I felt a weird sense of relief, as though I'd passed some hurdle, some rite of passage, and now I could relax. The cot I slept on seemed a little more comfortable all of a sudden; the concrete floors seemed a little less cold. Maybe I'd finally completely resigned myself to being incarcerated; maybe I'd just given up.

At the very least, I had a decent place to stay, at last—I couldn't overlook that fact. Nelson Place was so much better than Green Street; I got to take a shower and eat three square meals every day, and I slept well at night. With all this normal stuff, and without access to heroin and sleeping pills, I actually became healthy for the first time in my adult life.

Believe it or not, I was pretty much a model inmate, so much that I was actually put on the payroll. First, the guards had me typing up arrest records, which they dictated to me; the state paid me $1.25 a day for that service. I got to hear about some pretty awful stuff that way, let me tell you—rapes, robberies, murders—everything that every lowlife coming into the jail had done to get there. After a while, after listening to all these atrocities, I started to think that the things I'd done really hadn't been so bad after all. But then again, I still couldn't remember half of the things I supposedly did.

I remember one specific report that I had to type, about a guy who had killed his wife. As the officer told me what to write, he joked, "Hey, maybe I can take this guy home for dinner, to meet *my* wife!"

I laughed along with him, being the company guy and trying to stay in the good graces of those who controlled my bathing and eating privileges. I detested these men and their uniforms, and their shiny badges that seemed to make them think that they owned everyone and everything they saw.

But the longer I was there, the more I realized that there was a fine line between us inmates and those who guarded us. Not that we were all decent people, equals except for the different cards our lives had dealt us. Just the opposite, we were all criminals and liars, no matter which side of the bars we were on.

Case in point: I hung out with the Italian inmates in the jail and, for a while, I knew one who was a baker. When my birthday came around, he got wind of it and decided that he wanted to bake me a cake. He brought the idea up to one of the guards, and the guard was okay with it, on one condition: The baker had to give him two packs of cigarettes. Like the guard couldn't just walk down to the corner store and get his smokes whenever he pleased. That was an example of jailhouse extortion at its best.

Stephen, young and innocent.

The boys at a corner gas
station on Mt. Prospect
Ave. in Newark.
Left to Right: Carl, Gus,
Stephen and Rich.

Mug shot from Yardville Reception
and Correctional Facility.

Stephen, not so young
and not so innocent.

Christina and her dad, Stephen posing at her wedding reception.

Stephen's oldest daughter, Dana—the first real love of his life.

Stephen speaking at the annual Turning Point gala.

Christina and Michael with Donna and Stephen.

Left to right: Jolie; Jason; Donna and Stephen; the bride and groom, Christina and Michael; Jacque and Jason; Jocelyn and Stephen Jr.

Christina and her dad dancing to "Can you Feel the Love Tonight" at her wedding.

Donna and Stephen at Christina's church ceremony.

Stephen Sr. and Stephen Jr., joking at Christina's engagement party.

Chapter 32

While I was locked up all that time, I had no visitors and more importantly, no one sending me money, so I took pretty much any work the guards would give me.

On occasion, I got to stand in a lineup. Whenever a white guy was picked up for a crime, all of us who were the same color—all six of us in the entire jail—were brought down. Anyone who agreed to do this got two packs of cigarettes for his trouble—good payment for an easy piece of work.

Usually, doing a lineup was all fun and games—turn to the left, turn to the right, please say the phrase, "Gimme your purse, you old bag." One time, though, a lady picked me out as her attacker, and the whole thing went sour on me real fast. I had a really obvious alibi, thanks to the New Jersey correctional system, but it made me stop and think: What if someone *did* recognize me from something I'd done to them before I'd been incarcerated? Something that I didn't even remember? After that sobering experience, I never did another lineup again.

But that was okay—there were always other jobs for me. I continued typing arrest reports, and even cooked meals for the guards sometimes. And every night, after they emptied out the "bullpen"—the holding cell where they kept everyone until they were officially charged with something—I went in and cleaned it up for the next night's new recruits.

Now, the bullpen was just a waiting area, really; no one in there had been officially searched yet by any of the guards. After they were booked, they'd be stripped and searched for any contraband items on their persons, but before then, anything they had, they kept.

Of course, this meant that a lot of things got discarded in the bullpen, so that they would not be found upon later inspection. One night, while I was sweeping the cell out, I came across a little glass vial full of crack cocaine—though I didn't know what it was. I had missed the whole crack epidemic on the streets; I'd stuck with my heroin and pills and regular old cocaine and had never tried any of the new "fad" drugs that other people had gone crazy for. Picturing the desperate guy who'd dropped this stuff in the bullpen—getting rid of his stash before he was naked and in much bigger trouble—I flushed the vials down the toilet. No sense in making any waves if I didn't have to.

After a few months, I had the run of Nelson Place. I could come and go as I pleased, to an extent; I worked unsupervised until eleven or twelve every night and then, unguarded, all alone, I'd go on the elevator back to my own floor, where a guard would let me in to my cell.

I still did the reports and the cooking, but the guards came up with new tasks for me from time to time as well. For a while, they had me delivering mail to prisoners on every floor; this included packages from their families, which I had to open and inspect before handing out. People got interesting stuff sent to them in jail and without their even knowing it, I had a pretty good insight into their personal lives. I knew it would be a very bad idea to mention this to anyone, but as I gave out the goods, sometimes I had to bite my tongue to keep from saying things like, "Hey, nice nude photo your girlfriend sent you there," or, "Enjoy those cookies from your mom. I know I did!"

Overall, I was feeling pretty comfortable in jail. I had no bills to pay, no rent to worry about, no constant threat of arrest or death hanging over my head anymore. I learned, during that time, how well I do when I'm under lock and key. If I don't have the ability or means to destroy myself, I really, truly thrive.

Despite my relative freedom, however, the jail was still brutal. There were fights, and there was violence; to avoid it all, I kept to myself most of the time and didn't get too friendly with anyone. I knew that if I got in with someone who turned out to be an asshole, I'd get killed right along with him, or at least get into a fight and lose all my privileges because of it. If that happened, I'd surely be moved to a different floor of the jail, where I'd have to start back at the bottom of the food chain—another thing that could get me killed. Needless to stay, I stayed out of fights at all costs. I became a loner like my life depended on it.

The one and only time I saw a familiar (though not entirely friendly) face at the jail was the day my ex-wife Debbie showed up for an unannounced visit. Obviously, our time together was awkward, but she didn't waste any time beating around the bush: She wanted to talk about us getting back together.

Is she out of her mind? I thought, trying not to laugh out loud. *Does she not realize that I'm in JAIL?*

"No," was all I said, and the crestfallen look on her face—well, it did pretty much nothing to me. The truth was, I didn't want to hurt her or my girls ever again; I even thought that she'd probably be better off with another man. I'd realized somewhere along the way that I was incapable of loving anyone, because I didn't know how to; marriage—a good, solid relationship—was not something that came naturally to me. When we'd met, I'd seen in Debbie the normal life that I'd always wanted, and I'd taken advantage of that, but I had never really made it a part of me.

At the time, Debbie was working for some pretty high-powered attorneys, and she said that she could try to help me out in court. I considered it, but the truth was, I hoped that she couldn't do anything. My life was so incredibly fucked—I had *nothing*— that I wanted to stay in jail. Possibly for a long time. I had respect there, I wasn't a piece of garbage like I was on the streets. I thanked her, but declined her offer, and told her to go home.

Chapter 33

One morning—it was some time in 1984, and I had been at Nelson Place for eight or nine months—my cell door opened and a guard told me to get up and get ready for court.

"Shit, already?" I said, sitting up in my bed and looking down at my bright orange jumpsuit. "I got nothin' to wear."

The guard looked at me in silence for a minute. Then he waved a couple fingers at me, motioning to me to get up and follow him. I figured that he'd decided that he didn't give a shit what I wore, and just wanted to herd me down to the courthouse as quickly as possible.

But, instead, he took me into the room where the inmates' belongings were kept—the stuff they came in with, all their personal possessions. I was very familiar with this room as well as its contents, because I was often put in charge of taking these effects from the prisoners and storing them away. Being a jack-of-all-trades at Nelson Place, I now realized, had its advantages.

The guard let me into the room and told me I had five minutes, and that I should pick out something good to wear to court. Though there were no white-collar criminals housed there—most of what I found was jeans and T-shirts, grubby enough to stand up by themselves—I managed to piece together something resembling a suit. At least it wasn't orange.

The guard came back for me then and brought me to the bullpen, where I would wait to be transported to the courthouse, which was directly across the street from the jail. My public defender came in to prep me for what was to come; he told me to plead guilty, and he'd get me a five-year sentence for everything, with the time I'd already served counted in.

"You could be out in no time," he told me, and I laughed. Like I cared when the hell I would get out.

I still didn't really know all the gory details of what I'd done in that old house of mine—the things I'd done to get locked up in the first place. I had gotten that very brief rundown from my first attorney, and a slightly more detailed version from my current lawyer, but the whole thing was still pretty fuzzy in my mind. I actually had a few different public defenders along the way, but I only ever saw them in court, and none of them really told me anything about what was going to happen to me, or what was going on.

So when I got to the courtroom that day, I was pretty shocked at what went down. When I was led in by the guard, the place literally erupted. A whole gang in the back stood up and started shouting at me in Spanish; a woman in front stood up and lurched over the railing, trying to grab me. She was screaming her head off, and I later learned why: This was the woman I'd pulled out of the car and thrown on the ground. No wonder she wanted a piece of me so badly.

When I stood up before the judge, I was charged with breaking and entering and commandeering a vehicle—some very serious charges that would be even worse today. Breaking into a house and getting in bed with a woman? That's what we call sexual assault these days, and that part where I pulled the woman out of her car and drove off in it? That would be considered carjacking.

When the judge asked for my plea, I said, "Guilty to everything known and unknown," just as my attorney had told me to. This meant that I'd be covered for any future minor things that might pop up, namely any court dates that I had blown off in the past. I was afraid that there were still crimes they didn't get me for yet—things I didn't even know I had done—so this plea seemed like a good deal to me.

I found out then that my ex-wife had written a letter on my behalf after all, even though I'd told her not to; it seemed to have helped, if only a little, but still, I wasn't that grateful. I really hadn't wanted her to interfere.

Just as the public defender had predicted, the judge gave me one five-year sentence in the state prison for the two charges he'd read, plus some other sentences for some older charges that were still hanging around. He did agree to make them concurrent, and to recognize my time already served. The catch, though, was that if I messed up even once during my time in jail, I'd have to go back and serve *all* the time I was given, one long sentence after another. It was an incentive to keep my nose clean, but at the same time, I didn't really care if I would ever be free again.

When I got back to Nelson Place, I changed out of the monkey suit I'd borrowed from various other inmates and returned it to the property room. Then, I called my brother Vinny—collect, as usual—to let him know what was going on. His wife answered again, and I told her about the sentence. I also threw in a little sob story about how lonely I was, with no one visiting me and nothing to do. As far as she knew, all I did was sit around, watching other prisoners open their packages from home and crying in my state-issue bologna sandwich. She said she would talk to Vinny and see what they could do to help me out.

A few days later, I got my first and only piece of mail: a check from my sister-in-law, for fifty dollars, made out to my name. She had included a short letter: "God bless. See if this helps." I wasn't sure if it was a kind gesture or a blowoff. I probably would have handled it that way too, if I were her.

I showed the check to one of the guards. "What are you going to do with a check—*in jail?*" he asked me, laughing loud and long. When he was finally done, he told me to endorse it, and he'd go out and cash it for me and put it in my spending account.

I thought about this for a few minutes. What if I signed it over to him and he didn't come back with my money? I had no recourse, nothing I could do to him if he robbed me like that. But on the other hand... What the fuck would I do with this useless piece of paper, anyway?

So I signed it, and he took it. Surprisingly, the next day, I had fifty dollars in my jail account. I was more shocked by this than anything I'd seen in my life. This guy must have been the only good, honest person in the entire place, and that included me.

Chapter 34

In jail, all you've got is time: endless hours to sleep, to stare at the walls of your cell, to think about where you went wrong, to wonder when the hell they're ever going to let you out. In the days after my sentencing, I did all of that and then some, just waiting to find out which of New Jersey's many state prisons would be my home for the next five years.

The holdup was that none of the correctional system folks could decide quite what to do with me. I still had the Cadillac charges pending in Clifton, which was in a different county and thus on a different court schedule. Where they would put me for the long run, it seemed, might have depended on the outcome of that case. At least, that was what I figured. No one really told me much of anything.

I did know for sure, though, that there were other factors that could influence my placement—like my age, and the crimes I'd been convicted of. The powers-that-be took such things into consideration when deciding where to send an inmate so that they didn't end up housing a bad-check writer with an armed robber or a murderer. Seemed fair enough to me. And if that was what they were thinking about in my case, I could wait as long as it would take for them to come to a conclusion.

Finally, they decided to send me to the Yardville Reception and Correctional Facility, where they would hold me until they decided what prison to send me to. Maybe they had to make room for new guys at Nelson Place, I didn't know; all I did know was that I was not happy at all to leave. I was *someone* at Nelson Place, and I was about to become no one again—the low man on the totem pole, with no privileges and no friends. The prospect of being the new guy, of starting all over in a strange place, did not make me very optimistic.

I was taken out of Nelson Place on a Friday—the only day they transferred prisoners to other facilities. When it was time to leave, the guards brought me out of my cell and hooked me up to a long chain of shackled prisoners, handcuffing me to a short, bald, heavyset gentleman on one side and a tall, skinny black man on the other. They both scared me. I tried to just look down at my feet the whole time and pretend that they weren't there.

But, it seemed that my hair-challenged partner to the left had other plans. Though it was considered a disrespect of the highest order to ask another inmate what he was in jail for—it was something along the lines of discussing salaries with a coworker, except you'd get beaten severely for even mentioning it—this guy, for some reason, decided that I just *had* to know what he'd done.

"I met her," he growled near my ear, leaning in as far as his shackles would allow. I could feel his hot breath, his eyes boring into the side of my head. "I fucked her. And I killed her."

I cleared my throat and looked straight ahead, hoping to God that this psychopath wouldn't see my legs shaking. *Jesus Christ*, I thought as the guards began to lead us out to the bus. *All I did was do some drugs and steal some money from my cushy, white-collar job. Please don't put me in a cell with that guy!*

The vehicle that transported us to Yardville was just like a school bus, except with bars on the windows and state trooper vehicle escorts in the front and back. The ride there took an eternity, and I prayed the entire way that the wacko I was still handcuffed to wouldn't decide to tell me any more salient details of his criminal past. I continued to avoid looking at or anywhere near him, hoping to deter him from any further conversation.

Once we arrived at Yardville, we were herded off the bus, brought as a group into a large room and told to strip. Guards came in and placed an empty cardboard box in front of each of us, and gave us each a black permanent marker.

"Put your clothes in the box," a guard informed us, "and then use the marker to write on the box an address where your belongings can be sent."

I stood there in my underwear and miserably stared at the box at my feet. I gripped my marker tightly in my hand, wracking my brain for an address. *Any* address. Nothing came to mind.

"Write your address on the box," a guard told me. He was tall, skinny and black, like the guy I'd been handcuffed to on the way in.

"I can't," I said quietly, my head hanging.

"What do you mean you can't?"

I sighed, defeated yet again. Another blow to my already defeated ego; another reminder that in the outside world, I didn't exist. "I don't have an address," I told the guard.

"Any family you can send it to?" he asked. I couldn't even answer, I was so embarrassed. I just shook my head.

The guard bent over and picked up my box of clothes, and then took the marker out of my hand. When I looked up at him, he was shaking his head. "I'm gettin' more homeless white boys in here every week," he muttered as he walked away with the only belongings I had in the world. I never found out what he did with them.

Chapter 35

The time at Yardville did not pass any faster than it had at Nelson Place. I did a lot more of nothing there, a lot of sitting in my cell and wondering, *How did I get here?* I thought about my days at Cadillac, about what a big guy I'd been there—the boss, the man everyone had wanted to know. I thought about my marriage, and my two daughters, who had probably forgotten who I was. How did I go from having all that—everything I could want and then some—to sitting in a jail cell with nothing to my name, lamenting the sad fact that I'd no longer be the guards' favorite prisoner?

When I was finally called to straighten out the Cadillac charges in Clifton, the judge decided that since Essex County had given me the five-year deal, he would only fine me, with no additional jail time. It was a break and I knew it, and when he gave me the old, cliché "I hope you've learned your lesson" speech, I could almost, *almost* admit to myself that I had.

With this hearing came the final decision on my placement as well: The wise overseers in the criminal justice system decided to send me to Jones Farm, an offshoot of the New Jersey State Prison in Trenton.

Before I could go to the farm, I had to spend some time at the main prison facility, home of the state's death row population and more scary, violent inmates than I wanted to even think about. So much for keeping the low-level guys like me away from the lifers, the big-timers, the thugs who would grind me up and eat me for breakfast if given the chance.

Staring out the window of the bus as I headed toward Trenton, I felt more defeated than ever—and that's saying a lot, because it had been a long time since I'd had any sort of faith in myself. I didn't know what it was, but something about this new turn of events just felt like *it*, like the final step. I was going to fucking *prison*; this was for *real*. I was about to be totally and completely consumed by the system, and all I could do was throw my hands up and admit that I'd finally had it.

From the minute I saw Trenton State out the bus window, I was scared. The building looked like some sort of fortress left over from the Revolutionary War: all dark, old brick, high walls and turrets, everything surrounded by razor wire. It was like something from a nightmare, like the worst image from the harshest prison movie ever made.

Thankfully, I was quarantined for my entire stay. I was in a cell by myself for twenty-three hours a day and rarely saw—much less interacted with—any other inmates. I got this "privilege" because I was a nonviolent offender, because my only crimes were drug use and theft. I hadn't hurt or killed anyone, and the prison people didn't want me to be around anyone who had. Really, it was for my own good. I thought that this was a wise decision for them to make.

Jones Farm was a satellite of Trenton State, a kind of off-site jail facility where "short-timer" inmates could go to work and serve out their sentences. I fell into this category since I'd already done eight or nine months in the county jail, all of which counted toward my total time served. I didn't know how much longer I'd have to be in, but I guessed that it wouldn't be much; back then, for a five-year sentence, you could really end up doing only nine months or a year in total.

The place really was an actual, functional farm, with fields and animals and everything, and I was sent there to milk cows. Yes, *milk cows*—I get how funny that is. Given my upbringing in Newark, and my adult life in the suburbs of New Jersey, you can imagine just how much up close and personal contact I'd had with livestock—specifically, none. The only cow I knew anything about was Elsie, from the cheese commercials I'd seen as a kid.

But milking cows seemed better than working in a hot laundry room or slinging slop in the cafeteria or any of the other jobs I could have gotten at the main prison. At least I got some fresh air, and at least I wasn't in the fortress anymore. These were the things that I tried to keep in mind as I got out of bed every morning at three-thirty and headed down to the dairy building.

My daily responsibilities, aside from the cow milking, included baling hay and feeding pigs. Because I was the new guy, the supervisors—all civilians, not actual prison guards—really heaped the work on me, and I ran myself ragged to get it all done. As long as I did everything they told me to and didn't complain, they treated me okay. For the most part, I didn't mind the work. At least it helped to pass the time, much more than sitting in my cell and staring at the wall would have done.

Not long after I arrived at Jones Farm, I ran into a guy named Stanley, whom I'd gone to grade school with. He was there for a five-year sentence, too; he'd served a year already and really knew the ins and outs of the place. He introduced me to the other Italian guys at the farm and I got in pretty good with them, too, which considerably eased my tension about even being there.

Chapter 36

Sundays were visiting days at Jones Farm, and although no one ever came to see me, I looked forward to them anyway because Stanley always had somebody coming in to bring him stuff. His family came by every week with packages full of food—pastries, cold cuts, sausages, big Italian meals—and he shared all of it with me and the other Italian guys. We had a feast every week, thanks to Stanley.

I tried to stay out of trouble as much as possible. I did whatever the guards and supervisors told me to and I didn't start or participate in any sort of conflict—except for once. But, really, it wasn't my fault.

There was this guy, another inmate I just could not get along with. He was a huge, white supremacist Hell's Angel, and he didn't like me. To avoid problems, I just stayed away from him just like I stayed away from everyone else, but I could tell that he looked at me sometimes, like my very existence just bothered the shit out of him.

And so one day, he came up and gave me a piece of his mind. I don't remember what his complaint was, but you know, a guy like that, in prison, really doesn't need an excuse to bother whomever he wants. He came at me, and we stood face to face—I didn't back down and run away, as he probably expected me to do. Staring up at him, not saying a word, I was silently terrified that he would crush me with his gigantic fists.

But, he didn't. He just glared at me for a minute and then walked away. I stood there, watching him leave, and let out a long, slow breath, thinking of the huge amount of pain I just escaped because I had the balls to stand up to one of the baddest guys in the place. He could have demolished me in a minute, but for once, my stupid pride did me some good. Later, he got in trouble for drinking and was sent back to Trenton State, and I never saw him again.

There were many situations at the farm where I could have been killed and no one would have known—or cared, probably. Just like I'd seen before in my high school, in the methadone clinic, in jail and in the rehab I'd been to, Jones Farm had its share of racial problems between whites and blacks. There was a constant tension in the air, a threat of violence that sometimes came to an awful, brutal head. Inmates of both colors would get beaten up pretty badly, and they'd just be scooped up and brought to the hospital. The perpetrators would never be found, and just like it had been in Newark when I was a kid, nothing would ever be done about it. End of fucking story.

Jones Farm was a minimum-security facility, which meant that we were allowed to work independently, though we had to be counted by the guards periodically. Every hour, they blew their whistles and we inmates had to be front and center in a matter of seconds. Anyone who missed the roll call—even if it was just because he was in the bathroom or dozing off, even an honest mistake—got sent back to Trenton, no questions asked. I had to be on my toes all the time because going back was the last thing on earth that I wanted to do.

The threat of being returned to the state prison was a black cloud that had hung over my head since my first days at the farm, when a guard had told me that any one thing I did wrong—even some tiny, minor, accidental slip-up—would get me sent back. I thought about this every day, with every move I made. I'd seen enough of Trenton during the short time I'd spent there and knew that I never wanted to go back for any reason.

In fact, I didn't even want to go there to get looked at by a doctor when I was sick. Every morning, I watched other guys getting on the prison bus that would take them to Trenton to get medical or dental attention, and saw the armed guards surrounding them. It looked like a terrible experience, just to get a cavity filled or an aspirin for a headache. Even on days when my own mouth throbbed, or when I was so congested I could barely breathe, I vowed that I would never get on that bus. Not for anything. One time I even fell and injured my back, and I hid it from the guards so that they wouldn't send me to the doctors. Fortunately, they didn't notice my hobbling around, and I got better in a few days.

My aversion to the main prison served as a good motivator for me to do well at Jones Farm, and after learning the ropes of cow milking, I really excelled in my new profession. After about eight months, I went from pulling on udders all day to supervising the whole plant, and even delivering milk to other prisons including Rahway, which was similar to Trenton, and Clinton, the women's prison. As I rode up to that facility in the delivery truck, I'd often catch glimpses of the female inmates sunbathing during their yard time, and if I was lucky, one or two of them would flash me.

Other than those occasional shows, my opportunities to see women were, obviously, extremely limited. There were the regular Thursday night movies at the farm—I imagined there had to be some good-looking actresses in those, right?—but for some reason, none of the other inmates I was friends with ever wanted to go watch one.

"Fine," I told them one Thursday night, bored and desperate for something to do. "I'll go by myself."

So I marched it on over to the building where the movie was being shown; I found a seat in the packed room and waited for the show to start. When it did, it took me a few minutes, but then I realized—oh yeah, that was a porno they were showing.

What the fuck? I thought. Showing a porno movie to a roomful of male prison inmates? Were the guards *trying* to start a riot?

I got up and left—watching graphic sex scenes with a bunch of other men was just not my thing at all. I went and found

Stanley and the other Italian guys and when I told them what I'd seen, they all had a good laugh at my expense.

"Why didn't you tell me?" I asked. "That was just about the most uncomfortable three minutes of my life."

"I thought you'd want to see it!" Stanley said, laughing. "Besides, you want uncomfortable? You should've been here the night they showed *Mandingo*."

Chapter 37

The dairy building where I worked was next to a large, open space on the farm—an area of the grounds with no buildings and a clear view of the long road leading to the facility. On visiting days, every family, friend and loved one had to drive down that road to get to the farm. I watched them come and go sometimes as I worked.

Though it was a little hard to see from far away, one day, I noticed that every once in a while, things would come flying out the windows of these visitors' cars. I figured that they were just getting rid of some trash, and I went back to milking my cows, not really giving it a second thought.

But then, later on, an inmate came up to me with a proposition that made everything I'd seen a little clearer. Apparently, the things these people threw out of their car windows were for him, and apparently, they were not pieces of trash. They were tennis balls that had been cut open, and inside, there were bags of heroin and marijuana. The "visitors" threw them over the farm's fence and into this open field, and then the inmate's challenge was to find a way to retrieve them.

"You go get 'em for me," the guy told me, "and I'll give you some of what's inside."

I thought about it. I hadn't had any drugs for a while and for just a split second, the offer was tempting. But then, a vision of Trenton State Prison flashed across my mind, with its turrets and its barbed wire and its twenty-three-hour-a-day quarantine, and any good feelings I might have had about the situation quickly ran away in terror. I declined the inmate's offer. Nothing was worth the risk of getting sent back to Trenton—not even the possibility of getting high.

Overall, my time in prison wasn't so bad. It was scary sometimes, and boring an awful lot, but it wasn't as bad as I'd expected it to be. I worked hard, and I tried to keep myself out of trouble. I had no personal visits, no phone calls, no letters. I had burnt every possible bridge. In the middle of my incarceration, I was finally, finally free.

Since I'd given up on the possibility that anyone would visit me in prison, I was surprised one day when I was informed that some people had come to see me. Unfortunately, it turned out to be a couple of attorneys. They wanted to test my competency.

"My what?" I asked them, wondering why the hell they needed to know if I was sane or not. Wasn't that something that should have come *before* the trial and sentencing?

They explained that it had nothing to do with anything I'd done, had no relation to my crimes or my incarceration or any of that. It was just that my ex-wife could collect from Social Security if I was unable to take care of my own affairs anymore, and these guys had come to make that assessment.

I figured that the chances that I was not entirely with it were pretty good, because I'd noticed changes in myself lately that I could only attribute to all the years of drug abuse. Sometimes I couldn't complete sentences; often, I felt like I just couldn't think straight. Though I'd been a great baseball player as a kid, on the prison softball team, I missed pop flies because I couldn't judge where they would land; something in my depth perception had become all messed up.

So while I was thinking about inkblots and straightjackets, the lawyers had nothing so interesting in mind. They simply sat me down in a visiting room and asked me one inane question after another: "What day is it?" "Who is the president of the United States?" "What state are you in?" "What color is a light brown dog?" I tried not to laugh as I answered them, but I couldn't help trying to get them to admit that the whole thing was some kind of prank.

At the end of it all, to my great surprise, I was deemed legally sane and able to handle my own affairs, and the lawyers left me alone after that. Later on, however, another set of them came by on behalf of my ex-wife and got me to sign away all my rights to the property I'd owned with her. They told me it was the right thing to do, and I believed them. I think I even felt a little bit good about it.

The only other visit I had at Jones Farm was from a group of people who were running a new program called ISP—the Intensive Supervision Program. They told me that they would parole me out of prison early if I could get a place to live, maintain a job, stay away from alcohol and drugs, keep track of every nickel I spent, obey a curfew and submit to daily urine tests.

Sure, I thought. *Nothing to it!* I told them that I may as well stay in jail, to save us all the trouble.

But it did sound like a good opportunity, and so I agreed to give it a try, even though I didn't think that anyone would give me a place to live or a job. In fact, maybe that was *why* I agreed to it: because I didn't believe that it would really happen. In all honesty, I didn't look forward to getting out of prison, because I had nothing waiting for me—no home, no family, no job, no money, no self-respect. I had such a mountain of difficulties to overcome, being released was pretty much the least of my concerns.

But anyway, I set the process in motion and as with everything else having to do with incarceration, it was slow. I had to have patience. There were requirements that I had to meet, forms that had to be filed.

First, I had to go to a special hearing before three judges, who would hear testimony on my behalf from any friends or loved ones who cared to show up. Surprisingly, my ex-wife, my daughters and my brother Vinny were all there.

The judges asked Vinny if he would be able and willing to give me a place to live and work, if I were to be approved for this program, and he said yes.

They asked Debbie some questions, too. She was getting ready to marry another guy at the time, so I guessed that it meant a lot that she showed up for me that day. The air was tense—I wouldn't have expected it to be any other way, given the things I'd done to her in the past—but the guards and officers in the court did their best to keep things civil, to help us get along and make the whole thing easier on everyone.

At the end of the day, the judges agreed that I was a good candidate for the Intensive Supervision Program. They laid out all the rules for me again and warned me that any one infraction would land me right back in prison, serving out *all* my time—no concurrent sentences, no second chances.

Chapter 38

I was released from prison on June 13, 1986, and that night, I started working for my brother. Vinny owned a company that hired out bands for wedding receptions; I made my first sale with the first client I met, even though I had no idea what I was talking about. I may have been clean, but I was happy to find that I still had that old addict's charm to fall back on.

Though he'd said that he would give me a place to live once I was out on the streets again, Vinny didn't bring me to his house and put me up in the guest room or anything. Not that I could blame him—I wouldn't have wanted to be around me twenty-four hours a day, either. Instead, he set me up in a room at the Town and Campus hotel in West Orange. It cost a whopping fifty bucks a week, and it wasn't even worth that much. The place was a disaster, the room full of fleas and roaches, but I was used to that sort of living condition—and, at least, I wasn't in jail.

Immediately upon my release from Trenton State, I had been assigned a parole officer, a black woman whose name was, I think, Mrs. Williams. She didn't like me at all and let me know that whenever she could. From day one, she was on my case about everything, even going so far as to tell me that it was her goal in life to send me back to jail. She'd do it the first chance she got, she swore, and she would slam the cell door herself.

Maybe Mrs. Williams hated her job; maybe it was my personality she didn't like. Either way, her treatment of me wasn't right, but there was nothing I could do about it. She harassed me every day, and I just had to take it. She even showed up at my door at three in the morning sometimes, with a group of police officers.

They'd toss my room like a jail cell during a contraband inspection—emptying the dresser drawers, flipping the mattress, tearing the place up just because she felt like it.

A month into the program, Mrs. Williams almost got her wish to send me back to prison. One of my mandatory urine tests came back dirty for marijuana, which I hadn't touched. Mrs. Williams and her officers came to my hotel room and grilled me about it. "Just admit it," she said to me, "and we'll let you go."

Of course, I wasn't that stupid. I wouldn't admit that I'd done anything wrong, because I hadn't. Well, okay, I did have a drink once in a while, but come on, I had to have *some* fun and besides, that wasn't the issue at hand. When I wouldn't give in, Mrs. Williams and her band of enforcers left. I don't know if they were making the test results up or what, but strangely enough, I never heard anything about it again.

The next Thursday, I went to the ISP office in East Orange, as I did every week, for my regular check-in appointment. I was sitting in the waiting room, dreading my meeting with Mrs. Williams, when some guards with Trenton State Prison patches on their sleeves came in and put shackles on the guy sitting next to me. As they cuffed him, I overheard what they were talking to him about, and the gist of it? He'd had a dirty test result, and he'd admitted to smoking pot.

Jesus, I thought, slumping back in my chair. *That could have been me. They could have come for me.* A picture of Trenton State passed through my mind and I shuddered. Even though I'd been out of prison for a while by then, the place still gave me nightmares.

A few weeks later, another of my tests came back bad—this time for alcohol, a charge I couldn't refute. Mrs. Williams didn't interrogate me again but I when I was called to go before a panel of judges for review, she told me to bring my toothbrush, because I wouldn't be going home for quite a while. I knew that she was probably right.

On the day of my hearing, I showed up in court alone. I didn't even tell Vinny that I had to go; after all he'd done for me so far, I didn't want to disappoint him, or even to let him know that I'd fucked up. I figured that if I had to go back to prison, I'd call him from there and break the bad news.

To the great disappointment of my parole officer, however, the judges decided to give me a break and dismiss the charge—something that was pretty much unheard of in the Intensive Supervision Program, where every violator was sent back to jail no matter what. There was a high rate of recidivism in the program partially because the rules were so strict that no one could follow them to the letter, and partially because judicial leniency was non-existent. In this case, there truly had to be some sort of divine intervention on my side.

From then on, I really tried to keep my nose clean as much as possible. I stopped drinking, which turned my life miserable overnight. I showed up at the ISP office every week, like clockwork, for my mandatory check-in. I worked long hours and when I wasn't at the job, I was cocooned in my hole-in-the-wall, bug-infested hotel room. I lived like a hermit—no visitors, no friends—like I was still back in jail. I stayed under a self-imposed lock and key because it was the only way I knew how to keep from straying down a bad path again.

Chapter 39

On one visit to the parole office, I was sitting at Mrs. Williams' desk, answering all the standard questions, vowing that I had not used any drugs or alcohol and accounting for all of my time and money. At one point during the interview—which I had pretty much memorized by then and could probably have recited in my sleep—she had to leave the room for a few minutes. Being nosy, I leaned over her desk to see if I could check out any notes she may have written about me.

And that was when I saw it: the memo that changed my life. It was just lying there on the desk, right out on the open. "No longer screening for alcohol," it said, "only drugs, due to budgetary restrictions."

I let this news sink in to my brain as quietly as I could, even though the more I understood it, the more I wanted to get out of my chair and jump for joy. These were the best words I had ever read. I could drink! I could *legally* drink again! I felt renewed, like I had been given my life back, like I had gotten an official governmental pardon from a very long life sentence.

Now, the memo could have been fake, or about something else entirely. I had no idea if it pertained to me or the program I was on, but I was willing to gamble my freedom on it, because alcohol was, to me, more important. Anyway, I had no inclination to ponder any of these thoughts. I was too busy thinking about what my first celebratory drink was going to be.

Across the street from my seedy hotel home was a bar called Rascal's Comedy Club, and that night, after leaving the parole office, I headed right for it. I sat down at the bar and drank a couple of cranberry and vodkas, and talked to the other patrons like I'd been going there every night for twenty years and they were all my best friends.

And then, I went back the next day for a few drinks, and the day after that, and then it became my new regular haunt. I didn't feel bad about slipping back into the old habit because, I rationalized, it wasn't the *worst* habit I'd ever had. In the past, alcohol had just been a starter for me, the thing I'd used to loosen up with before getting into the really hard stuff, the pills and the heroin that I really wanted.

This time, though, I knew that I had the presence of mind not to let it go that far. This drinking was court-sanctioned, and I had no desire to do anything that was not within the parameters of my parole. I was so afraid of going back to jail that I didn't even think about pills or cocaine. I just drank, because it was the one legal fix that I could have.

And okay, so I drank a lot. But it didn't prevent me from sticking to the Intensive Supervision requirements. I met curfew, I accounted for my spending, I worked like a dog. I even went to recovery meetings—one AA and one NA per week. They were a stipulation of my parole, and I hadn't missed one since I'd gotten out of jail.

I didn't ever *want* to go to these meetings—why would I want to sit around and listen to people whine about how unhappy they were, when I could have been at happy hour at Rascal's instead?—but I went anyway, because I had to. I had a card that I had to get stamped, and then I had to show that to Mrs. Williams every week. One missed meeting, one slip-up, would have put me right back in jail, and you already know how I felt about that possibility.

I took buses to get to these meetings; as I got to know the other regulars, they offered me rides as well. I didn't have a car—couldn't afford one and anyway, it was probably for the best, as I often showed up for meetings full-on drunk. I was certainly not fit to be behind the wheel of any kind of vehicle most of the time.

I didn't pay a lot of attention at the meetings—I was not at all interested in recovery and attended only because I had to. Mostly, I used them as opportunities to catch up on some sleep, or to socialize.

Once, I was sitting in the back of a room, talking to a couple of girls, joking around and trying to charm the pants off them— so to speak, more or less. Even in that sad state, I was a charismatic guy, and I was working it.

In the middle of this, a guy came up and asked me to lead. As in, *lead the meeting*. I sputtered for a minute, taken aback, a little scared, but then I said, "Sure, why not?" I strode up to the front of the room and opened my mouth to make some big speech about how far I'd come or some bullshit like that—whatever sentiments I'd heard the other people making—but the guy followed me and cut me off before I could say a word.

"No," he told me. "I said leave. Not lead. LEAVE!"

If I'd been capable of embarrassment at that point in my life, I probably would have been red-faced, but instead, I just sauntered out of the room, winking at those girls on the way out. I had my stamped card in my pocket, and that was all I cared about. In fact, I was happy to be set free, and I got on a bus and headed back down to Rascal's for a nightcap before my curfew was up.

Chapter 40

Sometimes, God cuts you a break.

Even though I wasn't a very religious guy back then, that was pretty much how I felt when I found out that Mrs. Williams—the parole officer who hated my guts, who wanted to get me back in jail so, so badly—had suffered a brain aneurysm.

Okay, so maybe being happy about that wasn't very Christian of me, but I couldn't help feeling a little bit of relief that I would never have to see her again. And I didn't—either she'd gotten another job or died, I didn't know and I didn't care. I just knew that a huge weight had been lifted off my shoulders, and that it felt damned good.

The new officer that the parole board assigned me to was a good guy, so much better than Mrs. Williams had ever been. His name was Joe Urso—an Italian like myself, I thanked God for that, too—and I knew from the first time we met that he was an honest man. He wasn't looking to screw me; he never mentioned a desire to see me back behind bars. Instead, he treated me fairly, with compassion and understanding. He treated me like a human being. Now, I can honestly say that he was one of the reasons why I'm still alive today.

Joe did check up on me, like he was supposed to, but I never felt like he was trying to catch me doing something I wasn't supposed to do. He knew that I didn't follow the rules of ISP to the letter, but he just looked the other way on minor infractions, knowing that I could be doing much, much worse. He was kind, sympathetic; he talked to me about putting my life back together and he was so sincere about it that I actually took what he said to heart. Well, some of the time, anyway.

While I was on parole, I had no real contact with anyone but my brother. I had no friends, and no desire to make new ones; everyone I'd hung out with in the past was either dead, incarcerated or still doing drugs and thus off limits to me, because I didn't want to go back to jail. All I wanted to do was keep working, keep drinking and get through the Intensive Supervision Program as painlessly as possible. Beyond that, I had no plans.

And then, one night at Rascal's, Lisa the bartender, whom I'd become friendly with, introduced me to her friend Donna—another Donna, not the same one I'd been involved with before I'd gone to prison—and everything changed.

This new Donna and I hit it off, and we started meeting up at Rascal's for a drink here and there. She had a lot of good qualities—she was very stable, with lots of things I didn't have, like her own apartment, a steady job and a good credit rating—which made me wonder what she saw in me. I had to question why she wanted to keep spending time with me when there were plenty of better men she could hook up with.

I met up with Donna some nights when I got out of work, around ten o'clock, and we'd have a couple of drinks at Rascal's before I had to get back to the hotel. I explained to her early on that I was on parole, and let her in on a couple of the more obvious aspects of it—like the curfew, and the weekly visits to the parole office.

But, I didn't tell her everything. Not even close. I figured that if she knew all the limitations I had because of parole, she'd run away as fast as she could. What decent woman would want to be with a man who couldn't go outside a ten-block radius? Who had to ask permission for just about anything he wanted to do? None that I knew of. And so I kept most of that bullshit to myself. The less she knew, I figured, the better.

The way I got around that—how I kept Donna from knowing just how many restrictions I had on me—was to throw most of the rules out the window. I started breaking curfew and going places I shouldn't have—like New York, even though I wasn't supposed to leave the state. I thought that it was okay, though, because I had a girlfriend, I worked hard and I wasn't doing drugs, so I was entitled to bend the rules sometimes. And somehow, I never got busted for any of it.

I did come close from time to time, though. One night, we were sitting at the bar at Rascal's, having our nightly couple of drinks, and a bunch of people from the parole office walked in—including the woman who was in charge of the Intensive Supervision Program. As they came in, she looked me dead in the eyes, and my knees nearly gave out from under me. I couldn't tell if she recognized me or not, but just to be on the safe side, I turned to Donna and told her that we had to go.

"What? Why?" she asked as I led her out of the place by the arm. I didn't answer. I just kept pulling her along until we were safely inside my flea-infested hotel room, far away from the bar and the entire parole board inside it.

Joe Urso never said anything to me about that night, but I always expected him to; it was just another thing that hung over my head for all eternity, another *other shoe* that I expected to drop at any moment. At my next parole meeting, I was afraid that the Trenton State guards would show up with the shackles and haul me off. That was how they did it when you violated—they just showed up with no warning and took you away, like in a nightmare.

But, it never happened. Either those people who'd come into Rascal's hadn't recognized me or hadn't cared that they did, or they'd gotten too drunk that night and had forgotten all about me. Either way, it was a lucky break that I was never found out. And I was fine with that, because I figured I deserved one.

Chapter 41

As our relationship progressed, things between Donna and me were really good sometimes, and then they'd just suddenly go south—up and down, up and down, that's how we always were. But still, we stuck with it.

Sometimes, she told me I drank too much and she was probably right, but I still clung to my mantra: *I could be doing a lot worse*. I fought her on it every single time, insisting that I was fine, that I could handle my drinking, that it wasn't as bad as she thought it was. She'd be mad and I'd be mad, but we'd work it out and then things would be okay.

After we dated for about six months, she asked me to move in with her. Because I couldn't wrap my brain around the idea that maybe she loved me, I guessed that she was just tired of the bugs and the crazy people at the Town and Campus, and I couldn't blame her. It was no place for a woman to sleep. Hell, it was no place for a human being of any kind to sleep.

I had to ask the parole board for permission to move in with Donna, of course. They had to know every detail of our plans— what kind of money I'd be putting out, how I'd get to work, everything. She also had to meet with Joe Urso, but I wasn't worried about that at all. Donna was a nice, normal woman, and I knew that she would make a good impression.

When the day came, Joe went to look at the house where Donna and I would be living together, and without much investigation into the matter, he gave his okay. I guessed that he realized what I already had: that Donna would give me some stability. And we all knew how much I needed some of that in my life.

A year and a half later, I finally finished my parole. On my last visit to the office, I was informed that I'd "graduated"; they even gave me a certificate to show that I'd completed all of the program's requirements. Like I'd been going to college, and I'd earned a diploma that I could hang on the wall of my office to impress clients. As I took the piece of paper and shook Joe Urso's hand, I tried not to laugh.

That night, with the certificate folded up in my pocket, I went and played cards with some guys I knew. I also drank and did cocaine all night. What can I say? I had a good reason to celebrate.

And with that, I started the whole thing all over again—I went right back to all my old ways. I knew a guy in Rascal's who sold the old sleeping pills I loved so much, and I was right back on them immediately. I took them every single day, couldn't make it through a day without them. They were like a long-lost friend whom I'd finally gotten back in touch with after a long time apart. Everything now seemed like it was back to normal.

When my Rascal's dealer wasn't around, or when I just felt like getting out of town for a little while—now that I was off parole and *could* get out of town—I used my company car to go into Newark to buy drugs. I kept on working as much as ever, but I'd leave every day at lunchtime and have three or four drinks at Rascal's. When I went back to work in the afternoon, I always felt like I got a lot more done. I'd always believed that I was a better salesman when I had something running through my system.

I put in a long day every day, not leaving my office most nights until nine-thirty or ten o'clock. As I left, as I locked the door and walked out to my car, I'd pop a few pills in my mouth, getting a leg up on my high for the night. I had a ten- to fifteen-minute drive ahead of me—just enough time to race down Route 280 and get home before the drugs started taking effect.

In general, I tried to avoid being high while driving as much as possible. I did this not because I was so safety conscious, but because I really, *really* didn't want to get caught for DUI. If I got pulled over while I was high, I would go straight back to jail for sure, and even though I was doing the same old stupid shit again, jail was the absolute last place I wanted to go. It may not make sense, given my recurring drug use, but I would have done anything to avoid any further incarceration.

Most evenings, the pills would kick in just as I walked through the door of my house, if I'd timed it right. Once inside, I'd head right for the living room and crash out on the couch, where I'd slump over and try to enjoy the high.

I say "try to" because most nights, it was next to impossible, thanks to Donna's yelling. She always gave me a hard time when I was high; I can't blame her for it, but I certainly didn't like it at the time. I know that she felt sometimes like I was a lost cause, because nothing she said to me—or yelled at me—had any effect, mostly because I just didn't want to listen.

Basically, I was a drug addict, and nothing could change me. I was resigned to that sad fact, and as I drifted off to sleep to the sound of her frustrated shouting, I just wished that Donna would accept it, too.

Chapter 42

In the middle of all this, Donna got pregnant and not surprisingly, the news didn't inspire me to sober up. In fact, it didn't really faze me at all, in any way.

I did agree to marry her. It seemed like the right thing to do—and, more importantly, like something that I could do to keep her happy and, hopefully, off my back about other things that she liked to harass me about.

But, it didn't. In fact, I think that this new development in our relationship made her more determined than ever to get me onto a straight and narrow path. She'd never had a problem with telling me to stop my drinking and drugging, and now that she was pregnant, she felt as though she had even more of a right. "If you want to be a father to my child," she'd tell me, "you'd better get yourself cleaned up. I mean it."

Of course, this went in one of my ears and right out the other. To me, she just didn't know what she was talking about. I was handling everything fine; I would handle having a baby fine, too. I blew off her warnings and just kept on trucking, getting high every night and drinking as much as I wanted to.

And in time, understandably, this took a toll on Donna. One day, frustrated by everything I was doing and not doing, angry because I wouldn't listen to her at all, she flat-out told me that she could not have a baby with a man like me.

A man like me? I thought. *What the fuck is that supposed to mean?* I was absolutely floored. Was she saying that I was unfit to be a father? Was she questioning my manhood? In my mind, she was, and that was something that I never stood for—not from anybody. I didn't say anything to her at the time, didn't do anything that I would later regret, but I swore to myself that I'd kill her one day for saying what she had, and I meant it.

Needless to say, we did not proceed with our marriage plans. But, we did stay together, and that's a testament to the amount of patience Donna had with me, even though I knew that I just didn't deserve it a lot of the time. I believe now that despite everything, she really wanted to make some sort of family out of us—to have the baby and have me as its father. Somehow, she seemed to believe that it could actually happen.

Me, though, I just didn't think about it. Never in my life did I plan for my future; I was used to taking things as they came along, and this situation was no different. Today, she was pregnant; tomorrow, maybe she'd give birth, and then, we'd have a baby. After that, something else would happen, but damned if I had the coherence to figure out what it would be. I didn't think in big-picture terms.

But Donna did, and so she persisted with trying to help me with my "problem." She talked about quitting drinking, about getting clean, about rehab. When that word came up, I knew I was on the hot seat again, and as I usually did when I felt that sort of pressure, I caved. I gave in. I said what she wanted to hear so that she would leave me the hell alone and stop talking about it. I sort of agreed to maybe look into going to rehab. It wasn't a "yes," but it wasn't a "no," and that seemed to satisfy her for while. At least, it made her happy enough to want to marry me again.

Our wedding took place on September 4, 1988 and though Donna seemed happier after that, our new life together didn't take her mind off of the rehab idea. In fact, it seemed to make her even more gung-ho on the whole thing.

Donna had this friend Mary, who was basically my female equivalent. Our life stories were so much the same, except that where I had jail time, she had rehab at a place called Sunrise House, in Lafayette, New Jersey. When she got out, she started going to recovery meetings every day, got a good job and was getting herself together—she was really into turning her life around. Though I didn't relate to that part of her story very much, I had to admit that she *was* doing really well.

And of course, Donna looked at Mary and thought of me, and of the wonderful things that rehab could do for me, too. "Why don't you try what Mary did?" she asked me one day, and she sounded so optimistic that I couldn't give her another offhanded "maybe." This time, I told her I would do it.

Chapter 43

In November, I placed a call to Sunrise House from my office, in between appointments, with no real expectations and no clear outcome in mind. It was just something that I had promised Donna I would do, and so I was doing it.

An intake counselor answered my call. "What are you doing?" he asked me and in typical addict fashion, I lied. I told him that I was only having a couple of drinks a night, just to relax. Nothing more. I said this into the phone with a completely straight face. After so many years of doing it, dishonesty came very easily to me.

The counselor asked me around a thousand more questions. I could tell that he was trying to feel out just how much I was lying, and just how bad my problem really was. Finally, I guessed that he was satisfied with my answers—most of which were untrue— because he told me, "Okay, Steve. We have a bed for you. Why don't you come in today?"

Whoa, hold on a minute there, I thought. That was going way too fast. I'd figured that if I were going to actually go through with it—which I hadn't entirely decided on yet—I'd have time to prepare, to get my head ready for being locked up again. To at least have myself a little going-away party of some sort.

"But the holidays are coming up," I said. "I'd like to spend them with my family. Couldn't I go in January?"

The counselor then went on to list for me all the things that could happen to me if I waited that long to go into rehab: arrests, prison, overdoses, death. As he went on and on, my eyes rolled back in my head. Didn't he know how many times in my life I'd heard that lecture—and how little effect it had on me even the first time I'd heard it?

"Well, what do you think?" he finally asked. "Will you come in today?"

I laughed. "Yeah, sure," I said, and hung up the phone.

Though it was the middle of the day, I had a little time until my next appointment, so I headed across the street to Rascal's and had a few drinks, just to get the taste of the rehab conversation out of my mouth. *How fucking dare he*, I thought as I knocked back several glasses of the hard stuff. *He doesn't know me. How dare he tell me that I'm going to fucking DIE if I don't go in today? I'll go when I damn well please.*

The more I thought about it, the more angry and stressed out I got about the whole thing. Donna wanted me to go, and I kind of wanted to go so that she'd stop bothering me about it, but damn it, I had a life to live. I had a job to do, bills to pay. Didn't any of these people realize how hard it would be to just drop everything for twenty-eight days to go to fucking *rehab*?

The more worked up I got over it all, the more I wanted drugs and since my dealer at Rascal's wasn't there at that hour, I had no choice but to get in my company car and go to Newark. I drove down to Summer Ave.—my old hangout from back in the day, where I'd first started drinking, first started getting into trouble. It was more of a childhood home to me than any place else on earth. I returned there again and again as an adult, whenever I needed to forget that I was one.

I parked the car down the block from the building where I knew I could score my drugs for the day. Walking down the sidewalk, clutching a wad of cash inside my pocket and thinking about the relief the drugs would bring me, I noticed that there were birds singing. In the trees, all around me. Chirping and tweeting, like in a Disney movie. I distinctly remember the sound.

Coming up on the building, though, I started to hear another noise: footsteps, a lot of them, growing louder and louder. And as I was turning my head over my shoulder to see what was up, a mob of about a hundred cops came running up behind me. I stopped dead in my tracks and just let them go past. As they brushed by me, I wondered how I hadn't seen them when I'd gotten out of my car. It was like they'd snuck up on me all of a sudden, impossible though it seemed.

Once past me, the blue-suited swarm flew into the building I'd been heading for myself, undoubtedly on their way to an enormous, well-planned bust—the kind that would be on the 5:00 news. They were going to do this in the building where I regularly bought my drugs, where I consorted and did business with known criminals. Where I would have already been if I'd only hit one more green light on the way there.

My legs turned to jelly just thinking about it. How close had I just gotten to going back to jail? What kind of fucking luck did I have? Who was trying to send me a sign? I stood there for a minute, blankly looking at the building's door. And then I turned around, got back in my car and drove directly home.

When I got there, I called Sunrise House again. "I'll take the bed," I told the counselor. "I'll come in whenever you want me."

PART THREE

Chapter 44

Now don't get me wrong: The fact that I was going into a rehabilitation center didn't mean that I had any interest whatsoever in being rehabilitated. The thing that had happened in Newark—the dumb luck that had kept me from getting to that building five minutes earlier—had scared me, but not so much that it made me want to change my ways.

No, as usual, I was just going into rehab because I was feeling the heat a little too much, and because that big crowd of cops I'd encountered on Summer Ave. had been the last sign that it was time to get the hell out of town for a while. I told my drug dealers that I'd be back to see them in thirty days; I told my favorite bartenders that I was going on vacation and that I would be back soon. It didn't even occur to me that after rehab, I might not see—or *need* to see—these people ever again.

I'd only been married for a couple of months when I arrived at Sunrise House, at the urging of my wife and at the cost of her excellent health insurance plan. When I walked through the door and up to the front desk to check myself in, I was high from a handful of pills I'd taken that morning.

I had a good stash of pills hidden inside the collar of my shirt, too; I was tremendously addicted to them by then, and couldn't even fathom the idea of going without any for an entire month. I also knew that I would have to go through detox, and that the withdrawal would be, to say the least, unpleasant. I didn't want to be in any sort of discomfort, so I'd simply brought my own supplies to tide me over.

And, I was right—the detox did completely suck. Though I wasn't tied down to my bed like I had been at Skillman years before, the process they put me through at Sunrise House was still pretty brutal. They gave me a ton of medication to help me get through it, but I never felt like it was enough. And even with my own pills as supplements, I felt sick all the time. I lay in bed for hours with horrible chills running through my body—even with all my clothes on, plus a coat and a few blankets.

When the chills were done, I started sweating and vomiting severely. Add in the repeated trips to the bathroom, and I felt like my body was just losing control of its functions all at once. The detox went on for six very long days and I couldn't sleep through any of it, even though I was completely exhausted. What I'd thought would be a nice little vacation had quickly turned into a nightmare.

When I was finally done with that phase of my treatment, I was allowed out into the general population with all the other patients, and that was when the "program" really began. Whereas at Skillman, they had let me just sit around and watch TV all day, at Sunrise House, there was a strict routine: Wake up, take a shower, eat breakfast, go to groups until lunchtime, eat, go to groups until dinner, eat again, go to a twelve-step meeting at night. I had to be in my room and in bed by eleven, no exceptions. It was kind of like being in boot camp, just without the calisthenics.

One of the big parts of the recovery process—the very first part of it, matter of fact—is admitting that you have a problem. At Sunrise House, that amounted to announcing, to whoever wanted to hear it, that you were a drug addict or an alcoholic— or, if you were me, both.

Now, I had no problem admitting that I was a drug addict. I *was* one. That was a fact that I could not get around. However, for the first three weeks I was in rehab, I would not say that I was an alcoholic. In my mind, a drinker was somehow lower on the food chain than a pill popper like myself; to me, drinking *as an addiction* was somehow less cool, less acceptable than using other drugs.

Simply put, I didn't want to be known as an alcoholic. The only image that word conjured in my mind was of an old man standing by a trashcan fire, with a paper-bagged bottle in his hand, dirty, scruffy and talking to himself. That, I thought, was as far from me as it could get.

Back in the jail at Nelson Place, I'd been the guards' favorite, the go-to guy for any menial job they wanted done. At Jones Farm, I'd advanced far enough to be manager of the dairy building, and then released early under Intensive Supervision—a program that they didn't let just anyone take advantage of.

And now, locked up once more, shut away from the rest of the world and all its bad influences, I again rose to the top of my class without a whole lot of effort. I did well in the groups I attended; I participated in the meetings; I was just generally well liked by all my counselors and peers. Blame it on my addict's charisma—I could always pull out the charm when I needed it.

But of course, none of this meant that I was actually battling my addictions. If I was doing well in groups, it wasn't because I believed what the counselors preached to me; if I impressed people at meetings, it wasn't because what I said was so heartfelt. It may have *seemed* sincere, but really, I was just going along with it all because I was there, and I had nothing else to do—not because I believed in any of it. Recovery jargon passed in and out of my head all day, every day, and yet none of it stuck. I still didn't have any thoughts about quitting.

But then again, I wasn't thinking about using drugs again once I got out, either. I just wasn't thinking of anything, one way or the other. I had no plans for the future. Would I keep using? Maybe. Would I stay away from drugs forever? Maybe, too. I wasn't looking that far in advance. As always, I was just taking everything one day at a time and figuring that whatever was going to happen in the future was not something that I had to worry about yet.

The fact that I was just feeling so damned *good* might have had something to do with this relaxed attitude. In a setting like that, where everything was so controlled and focused, I had no responsibilities, really—no stress, no worries hanging over my head. I didn't have to think about work, or my marriage, or my family, or when I was going to use drugs again. My wife had even been instructed not to bother me with any talk about bills or problems at home. All I had to do was get out of bed, eat my meals, go to meetings and go back to bed at night. It was a simple existence, and I liked it.

Chapter 45

After a few weeks, the other patients at Sunrise House elected me their mayor. No kidding—I was literally *the mayor of rehab*. With this office came the great responsibilities of deciding which movies we would watch on the community TV and what toppings we wanted to order on pizza night. A new mayor was chosen every week, but my brief time in the spotlight sure made me feel special.

Around that time, I also started to introduce myself differently at meetings: "My name is Steve," I would say, "and I'm a drug addict and an alcoholic." I did this not because I was finally admitting that I had a problem, but because I wanted to please the counselors. Even after going through the terrible detox and being thrown into one self-help group after another, I still had no concept of recovery. I was just going along with the program, telling them what they wanted to hear in order to make things easier on myself. The more I conformed, the less they bothered me, and that was a formula I could work with.

But, I wouldn't say that I abided by every regulation they had—particularly not the golden rule: There will be no "he-ing and she-ing" in rehab. Most facilities like Sunrise House worked hard to keep male and female patients from socializing outside of groups, on the basis that consorting with the opposite sex was a distraction, and nothing should take one's attention away from recovery.

Okay, I could agree with that. I could see where they were coming from. But since I had no interest in recovery anyway, I just didn't think that the rule applied to me. I'd always gravitated more toward women than men for some reason, and in rehab, things were no different. If I was going to make friends, they were going to be female, and that was that.

In the groups, there were people who seemed to latch on to me, because, they explained, they liked what I had to say. Once, one of them left a note for me under my door. "You're special," it read. "I wish you luck in recovery. I know you have what it takes to be a counselor one day."

Me? A counselor? I thought, laughing to myself. *Are they all crazy here?*

While I was taking it easy over at Sunrise House, Donna was back at our place in West Orange, going through her pregnancy alone, paying our bills, handling every problem and spending Thanksgiving and Christmas on her own.

I knew that she could have been mad at me for leaving her by herself at a time like that, but just the opposite, she was my biggest supporter. She came to see me every Sunday, no matter what, and was never anything but happy and encouraging during our visits.

Seeing Donna once a week meant everything to me; it was the only thing I ever looked forward to in that place. Even though I really wasn't taking any of the recovery business seriously, I was sincerely grateful for her loyalty and compassion. I don't know how I got those two concepts to coexist in my head, but somehow, I managed to appreciate what she was doing for me even though I didn't really care about any of it.

When I'd gone into rehab, I'd had to take a sort of leave of absence from my job—on short notice, too, so you can imagine how thrilled Vinny was about the whole thing. I'd really put him in a bad position because I'd been making a lot of sales for him, and that meant that a lot of money just wasn't being generated if I wasn't there.

I thought about this the whole time I was in Sunrise House, and for a while, I felt bad about it. I remembered, of course, how he'd given me a leg up when I'd gotten out of prison, and I felt like I owed him for that, even though he never acted like I did. He also never mentioned how disappointed he was to learn that I'd returned to my old, bad ways, but I knew how he must have felt. I wouldn't have blamed him if he didn't want to give me my job back when I got out of rehab.

But then, as usual, my pompous ego took over, and all that sentimental bullshit went right out the window. If he told me that he wouldn't take me back, I figured, hey—it was probably for the best. I didn't really want to work with him forever, anyway. In fact, I knew that I could probably do better for myself somewhere else. I didn't know *where* else, and I didn't know doing what, but I had a lot of time to think in rehab, and I was sure that I could figure something out.

During my last week at Sunrise House, the counselors started talking to me about extending my stay for another twelve days. They said that I was doing *so* well, and that it would surely benefit me even further to keep going a little longer. That just a little more time would *really* help me prepare for living a clean life in the outside world.

Maybe I was just a cynic, but I knew that the only benefit they were looking for was the one that would come in the form of a check from my insurance company. They said themselves that I'd done the program well, so what on earth would another almost two weeks do for me?

But anyway, I agreed to stay. Hell, another twelve days to avoid reality? How could I say no to that?

At least, that was what I'd thought at the time. Now, in retrospect, I can see that maybe it was some sort of sign. Maybe there was a reason why I wasn't supposed to leave just yet. And maybe, it was some sort of higher power that was telling me that I should say "yes" to the invitation.

The reason I say all that is because during that extra time, during that extended part of my stay, something truly miraculous and completely inexplicable happened: I got it in my head that I want to give sobriety a try. I know, it sounds crazy. When it first occurred to me, I figured that I was losing my mind a little bit. *Me? Get clean?* I asked myself over and over, the words sounding foreign and uncomfortable in my head. I'd been so resistant to rehabilitation throughout my entire life that the concept barely held any meaning for me anymore.

But the idea persisted, as much as I tried to ignore it. It wouldn't go away and after a while, I had to just stop and consider it. I had to acknowledge that the way I'd been thinking, acting and living all along just wasn't working out anymore, and that it was time for me to give something else a try. I knew that I had to start actually listening to the Sunrise House counselors, and letting them help me for real.

I understood then, and I still believe now, how funny it was that after all the warnings I'd had before—arrests, jail time, near-death experiences and the loss of so many loved ones from my life—this was what got me to finally change: nothing. No threats, no ultimatums, no legally enforced penalties. Just a thought that occurred to me, an idea in my head. It's proof, I suppose, that timing really is everything.

Chapter 46

The winter holiday season is supposed to be a time of togetherness with loved ones, of shopping and wrapping and going to parties and getting loaded. If you were me, the holiday spirit also included giving little bonuses to your favorite bartenders, and stocking up on drugs for those long nights you'd have to spend at home with your family.

At least, that was how I'd spent previous Christmases. This particular year, since I was still sequestered in Sunrise House, however, things were a little different. There were no parties—not any good ones, anyway—and the only family I saw was Donna, who came to spend Christmas Day with me. She brought gifts and, God bless her, she tried to make the whole thing festive, but it was really just sort of depressing. I was in rehab, and I was sober on Christmas. What the fuck did I have to be happy about?

New Year's Eve was even worse, of course, because who wants to be in rehab on the biggest party night of the year? I spent the occasion sitting around and feeling sorry for myself, giving the evil eye to other patients who seemed thrilled to be wearing their little paper hats and blowing those irritating noisemakers. It was nice that they were enjoying themselves, drinking their soda and juice, but what I wouldn't have given for a good, stiff shot.

I pictured everyone else in the world—*everyone* else, in the *whole* world—out on the town, partying, drinking, doing drugs, having fun, while I was locked up there. It just didn't seem fair. Yes, I knew that I'd made the right decision when I'd chosen to not do any of those things anymore, but it didn't mean that I wouldn't miss them.

It seemed to me that sobriety, when I first chose to pursue it, should have been something more than it was. Every day should have felt like a miracle; every moment should have brought a revelation to my newly clear mind. There should have been epiphanies and rapture, and everything should have made sense at last.

Unfortunately, that just wasn't how it happened for me. There were no angels singing to me from on high when I woke up every morning; in fact, most days, I was groggy as hell. I didn't whistle a happy tune as I showered or have lively, jovial conversations with my tablemates over breakfast. I went to meetings and I participated as usual, but that was all the same, too, except that now, I kind of meant what I said a little bit more. At night, I went back to bed without the satisfied feeling that I thought I should have since I'd gone through another blessed day on this earth without picking up a drink or a drug.

No, instead, everything went on pretty much just the same as it had before I'd decided to go sober. I followed the regular routine and I met with my counselors every day, both in the groups and our one-on-one sessions; the only thing new about it was that they all seemed so proud of me for finally turning things around. "If anyone could do it, you could," one of them told me, and I knew he was right.

If nothing else, I was stubborn and when I decided to do something, I would take it all the way to the end. I didn't know quite how I was going to do that in this situation, but as usual, I tried not to worry about it. I figured that something would come to me.

I was released from Sunrise House on January 21, 1989. There were no more delays, no more invitations to stay on another week. Finally, I had to go out into the world and face whatever came at me with nothing in my system but a little hard-won luck and determination. To say that it felt a little daunting would be an understatement.

In the end, I'd "graduated" from the rehab program with honors; I guess that my last-minute turnaround had really impressed the counselors. As I left the place, many of them came to shake my hand and wish me luck on my new journey. They all seemed to have a lot of faith that I would keep up the good work once I was released. I hoped that they were right.

As a send-off from the program, I was given a set of marbles to keep in my pocket, as a sort of touchstone to use anytime I felt like drinking or using a drug. Literally, they were a reminder that I'd "lost my marbles" but had found them again. It was cute, I thought, and maybe a little silly, but at that point, I was willing to give anything a try.

Donna came to pick me up when I was released from rehab and, as usual, I was so thankful to see her. She was really pregnant by then and the drive there had been so uncomfortable for her, she asked if I would take the wheel for the ride home.

"Of course," I told her. I was willing to do anything to show my gratitude for her sticking by me for so long, through so much of the stupid bullshit that I'd done.

So we got in the car, and I headed toward home. I was excited to get back to my own apartment, my own bed. Sunrise House was comfortable enough but I was tired of being away; I wanted to be in a familiar place again while I figured out how I was going to keep this sobriety thing going for the rest of my life.

But after driving for a few minutes, something just started to feel wrong. My mind started racing, my heart beating too fast; I was sweating and shaking, like I was about to have a heart attack or something. I had to pull the car over to the side of the road before I crashed into something and killed us.

After a few deep breaths, I was able to compose myself, which I was thankful for—apparently, it wasn't a heart attack. I guessed that I was just overwhelmed, even scared maybe of being out in the big, bad world with nothing in my system. I felt like an exposed nerve—touchy, scared, jumpy, tense.

After that, I was afraid to drive and though I didn't want to do it, I had to ask Donna to take us home. As she drove along, I leaned my head against the cold glass of the passenger side window and closed my eyes, thinking about the hard time ahead of me. Whatever I was in for, I knew that it was going to be rough. I hoped that sobriety would be worth it.

Later that day, as I had been directed to before I'd left Sunrise House, I went to a twelve-step meeting. I found one in Essex Fells, not too far from where Donna and I were living; she dropped me off and I walked into the room alone and more unsure of myself than I had ever been in my life.

This was no joke, as going to meetings had been for me while on parole. I had no card to stamp, no quota to meet so that I wouldn't get sent back to jail. Daily meeting attendance was merely a suggestion, something that I should do for my own good, not because someone told me I had to. In going to this first meeting, I was willingly doing something that was good for myself *simply because it was good for me*—a concept that just left me terrified.

At this meeting, as the Sunrise House counselors had told me to, I raised my hand and announced that I was newly sober, that I'd just gotten out of rehab and that I needed help. It was difficult for me to say this, especially the last part—asking for help was not something I was used to, and it certainly did not come naturally to me. I could barely get the words out of my mouth above a mumble.

But even so, the response that I got from the other people at the meeting was overwhelming—and not entirely in a good way. The attendees were mostly men, and it seemed like a flood of them came over to shake my hand and talk to me about my story. Some even hugged me, which really freaked me out. As expressive and affectionate as Italians are supposed to be, I was never big on physical contact with anyone; my brothers had always hugged each other, but that had just never been my style. I had my tough image to protect, and a guard that I had to keep up at all times so that no one would actually get inside and see the real me.

But at this meeting, it didn't seem like I had a choice in the matter. These guys were practically lining up to congratulate me, like I was some sort of celebrity, and turning down their demonstrations seemed like it would be insulting. They were accepting me into their fold, no questions asked. For a minute, it felt like I'd fallen asleep and woken up on an entirely different planet.

Chapter 47

It didn't take me long to figure out that without anything in my system, life was very, very different and, honestly, I had a lot of trouble adjusting. I was so used to thinking and feeling in a certain way—with my mind always on drugs, with everything in my life revolving around buying them and using them—that when I was forced to do it sober, I just plain couldn't function. When I walked, I felt like my feet were on wrong; when I talked, my lips seemed to spout nothing but gibberish. I'd already proven that driving a car—sober, no less—I was a danger to myself and others. And when people talked to me, no matter how well I knew them, I had trouble looking them in the face. Everything just felt *wrong*.

In short, I felt like a completely different person, one with no character, just a nameless stranger adrift in a sea of other strangers. Without my old friends alcohol and drugs, I had no lifeline tethering me to the shore, showing me where to go to be safe. "Sober" means "Son Of a Bitch, Everything's Real," I heard someone say at a meeting once, and that was exactly how I felt all the time now. I was an addict with nothing to abuse. I just didn't know what I was supposed to do.

But instead of using that as an excuse to fall back into old, destructive patterns of behavior, I knew that I had to adopt a whole new way of living; basically, I had to start from scratch. I had to learn how to live the right way—the way I should have learned from the beginning. I didn't know who was going to teach me all this, or if I was going to have to teach myself, but I knew in my heart that it was the only option I had, if I wanted to succeed. Needless to say, the proposition was pretty fucking daunting.

As I was embarking on this quest to make a new life for myself, my wife, Donna, brought a new life into the world as well: She gave birth to our son Stephen on February 28, 1989. Though I'd been pretty ambivalent about becoming a father before I'd become such a changed man, once I held this tiny baby in my hands, I couldn't imagine feeling anything but love for him ever again. I was proud, and happy, but also scared; how was I supposed to teach my son right from wrong when I was only just starting to learn about such things myself?

But, I reasoned, he had never seen me drunk or high or out of control, and he never would, and that was a good enough start. I didn't really know how to be a father—I'd had the chance before and had messed it up horribly—and I was determined to do it right this time from the beginning.

Everything, though, was not so bright and shiny and optimistic all the time. Being sober was proving to be very tough. I had to change literally everything about my life—the things I did, the places I went, the people I hung out with—so that I wouldn't be putting myself back into any familiar situations, ones that might tempt me to return to my former ways. It was difficult, doing everything different, but I just had to keep reminding myself that my life was better now—that it had started to get better the day I'd put the cork in the bottle and left the drugs alone. And that the struggle it took to keep it that way was worth it.

Unfortunately, my body didn't entirely agree. With all the hypervigilance it took to keep my new lifestyle afloat came anxiety like you wouldn't believe, and it was almost no surprise to me that after a while, I started having panic attacks. Just out of nowhere, I'd feel like I was suffocating, like I was going to choke up and die. I felt claustrophobic even in open spaces and stressed out all the time, with no outlet. I felt, sometimes, like maybe sobriety was killing me.

So I went to a doctor to have a physical exam—something I couldn't remember ever doing before. I also went to see a dentist around the same time, as many of my teeth were falling out. I'd never taken care of my health in any way, because I hadn't really known that I should; it was another thing I'd never been taught as a kid, due to the situation my parents had been stuck in, with my mom's illness. But again, I don't blame them.

But I went to see this doctor for my panic attacks, and to see what else might be hiding in my body, ready to kill me at any moment. He poked and prodded me for a while, and listened to me breathe and checked my blood pressure and did all sorts of things that just seemed really strange to me. When I started to explain the panic attacks to him, the first thing he did was ask me how much coffee I drank and how many cigarettes I smoked on a daily basis.

"Oh, about forty cups and three," I replied, like it was the most sensible answer in the world. I didn't think there was anything *wrong* with the amount of coffee and cigarettes I consumed on a daily basis, but it was obvious that I was addicted to caffeine and nicotine. I just figured that at least they weren't drugs; they weren't illegal, or something that could kill me.

The doctor just looked at me for a minute. "You might want to cut down on both of those," he said finally. "It would probably help."

And with that, he went on to give me a clean bill of health. Nothing was physically wrong with me, he said. I was so surprised that my insides weren't just eating themselves alive that I thought he might be lying. It made me wonder if I should get a second opinion, for surely, there had to be something very wrong with me.

To be on the safe side, I cut down on the coffee and cigarettes, but fortunately, by then, I had something else to lean on: my job. I had gone back to working with Vinny when I'd gotten out of Sunrise House, despite my big ideas while I was in there that I could do so much better without him. The truth was, I couldn't, and I knew it. We worked well together, and I was good at the job. My doing it was a benefit to us both.

It was wedding season when I got out of rehab, so there was plenty of work to keep me busy; it was actually the company's biggest month of the year, and I was constantly on the run, meeting with potential clients and making lots of sales. I was so busy, I didn't even have time to think about drinking or using drugs, and I was thankful for that.

But then, as usually happens when things seem to be going really well, an event came up that put me in a bit of a compromising position. I had to do a show, for work, in a club where alcohol would be served, and just the thought of being in the presence of a bar made my heart race. I knew I couldn't be trusted to stay on the good path with that much temptation right in front of me. It was much too soon to ask for that sort of will power.

So, I told Vinny that I couldn't do it. I just plain flat-out refused. I told him that I was afraid that I'd start drinking again, and that my forty-two days of rehab would go down the drain, and that all the work I'd done since then too would have been for nothing. I knew that if I had just one drink, I'd end up in Newark, buying drugs and letting everyone I knew down yet again.

Vinny, as you can imagine, was not entirely pleased with my decision. I understood that really, he was just looking at it from a business perspective; this was a job responsibility that I was refusing to fulfill, and if I didn't do it, he'd be hard pressed to find someone who could. I felt bad about that, but I felt a lot more strongly that I had to do what was right for my *life*, not just for my job. This decision was more important than a career could ever be for me, and I stuck to it. I didn't go to the show, and I kept myself out of harm's way for one more day.

In the end, though it caused a momentary rift between my brother and me, I was glad that I did what I did. I know now that any success I've had since then, and the way I live today, had been because of those decisions I made in the beginning, when I was just learning how to live a normal life for real.

Chapter 48

When I left Sunrise House, I didn't really leave. I may have been out in the world, going about my business, but I wasn't really free—I still had to go to aftercare meetings for eleven weeks.

Really, aftercare was a good thing. It was sort of an added reinforcement, a way for the counselors to keep checking up on me, to keep me accountable for my actions. Actually, it was kind of like being on parole, except without the urine tests and the threat of going back to jail if I screwed up.

Aftercare was a regular part of the program for everyone who went to Sunrise House, and so every Saturday morning, I saw everyone I had "graduated" with. It was nice to catch up on what they were going through and see how they were doing. It was sad, though, to see the group getting smaller and smaller each week, as fewer and fewer of us showed up. Each meeting, the counselors would let us know who had died of an overdose in the last week, or who had been arrested and gone back to jail. It seemed to me sometimes like I was really beating the odds; the fact that I kept showing up for the meetings was my proof.

Aside from the group, we each had to meet with our individual counselors and tell them all the gory details of what we'd been doing on our own to further our recovery process. Again, this was a lot like parole; by the third or fourth week, I'd memorized most of the questions my counselor asked.

First, there was, "Are you going to meetings every day?" I was. Sometimes twice, if I felt like it.

Next, there was, "Have you found a sponsor yet?"

Most people in recovery have what is called a sponsor—a person they can call when they're feeling bad or need advice, someone they can rely on to help them figure out how to do the right thing and to guide them through the twelve steps of recovery. Usually, you'll find your sponsor in a recovery meeting. It's kind of like, you see someone you think you'd get along with, you ask that person to be your sponsor and hopefully, he says yes.

Now, I had not even approached anyone about being my sponsor during the several weeks I'd been going to meetings. It wasn't that I didn't think I needed one; as I already mentioned, I just didn't like asking people for help. At least, that was what I told the aftercare counselor at Sunrise House.

The bigger problem with the whole sponsor thing was that I would go to all these meetings, and I would listen to people tell their stories, and I would not relate to a single one of them. I felt like none of them had problems like I'd had. These were businessmen, professionals, successful people who had a few too many drinks after dinner some nights. None of them had been homeless. If any of them had been in prison, they certainly didn't mention it. How could I turn to someone for help, I wondered, if no one even understood what I'd been through?

But this, I knew, was not what my counselor at Sunrise House wanted to hear. So, every week at my aftercare meeting, I made up a new excuse as to why I hadn't found a sponsor yet. "I'm shy," I told him one week. "I have trouble talking to people," I said another. "I wanted to ask this one guy, but I didn't get a chance before he left." I was pretty sure that he didn't believe any of it, but he just politely reminded me that it was something I had to work on, and we left it at that until the next week, when I would give him another excuse.

Despite my reluctance to fully immerse myself in the recovery process—namely, my aversion to having a sponsor—I understood right from the beginning that I had to be totally vigilant in everything I did. I could drink or use drugs at any time; the temptation was always there, in my own mind. Whether or not I fell back into it was entirely my choice, and my life hung in the balance of this decision every single day.

During all those years when I'd been high and drunk and homeless and in jail, I hadn't thought about that choice. Hell, I hadn't even really known that it had existed. I'd drank; I'd taken drugs; that was all there had been to it. It was all I'd known and there had been no other way for me to get by.

In recovery, though, I reminded myself constantly of the choices I had to make. Going to a meeting every day? A choice. Being there when my wife or child needed me? A choice. Not drinking, using drugs or committing crimes? Choice, choice, choice, and I took each one as seriously as the next. I really applied myself to doing what it took to stay sober, to keep myself on the right path. It was a tremendous miracle that I managed to make good choices every day. Sometimes, it really wasn't easy.

Chapter 49

Deep down, I knew that even though I was doing everything else I had to for my recovery, I would never get anywhere without the support of a sponsor. It was how the twelve-step program worked and if I wanted it to work for me, I had to follow its rules. I didn't entirely like it, but I knew that I had to give it a try.

So I really started paying attention to what other people were saying at meetings. I scoured the crowds, looking and listening for the one person I could relate to. Believe it or not, even in those rooms full of recovering addicts and alcoholics, that was really hard to find. I still felt a little bit like an outsider, like no one else had been through exactly what I had, like no one was quite as *bad* as I was. I'd sit in the meetings, look around myself and think, *I just don't belong here.* I was far worse than any of those people, even though they were all probably thinking the same thing about themselves. We're all our own worst critics in the end.

And then, just like fate, I found the perfect guy to be my sponsor. His name was Brian, and one night at a meeting, he shared some stories about his past, which seemed to be sort of like mine. *Finally*, I thought, feeling a little relieved that there was at least one sort-of-kindred spirit there with me.

I bucked up my courage and asked Brian to be my sponsor and, thank God, he said "yes" right away. Asking had been hard enough; if I'd had to explain why I'd chosen him, I probably just would have run out of the place and gone home.

As I'd expected—and dreaded—Brian's first "assignment" for me was to start calling him every day. Every stinking day, I had to pick up the phone and give him a ring, just to let him know that

I was still around, still committed to recovery. It was a basic sponsor request, something that most people who had one had to do.

"Sure," I said to him. "Okay," as if I were perfectly at ease with his request. Inside, though, I was freaking out a little bit. *Call him every day?* I thought. *What, are we dating?* There was nothing natural to me about picking up the phone and calling a man just to shoot the breeze; I might have done it with a woman in the past, but a guy? If we had anything to say to each other, we could do it face to face. That was the way I'd always operated, and it made this one little task seem like a mountain-sized challenge—and one that I had to climb if I wanted to stay on the road to recovery.

So the next day, I started with the regular phone calls. I kept our conversations as short and sweet as he would let me: hi, everything's okay, see you at the next meeting, bye. Sometimes he tried to get me to talk more, but he was never really pushy about it, which I appreciated.

I got used to the phone calls after a while, but it wasn't really turning into something I enjoyed, like I thought it was supposed to. In fact, every time I picked up the phone and dialed Brian's number, I hoped that his answering machine would pick up, that he wouldn't be home, that he'd be asleep or in the shower, and that he would never call me back. I wanted his help, I guess, but I didn't want to have to talk to him about my feelings to get it.

Brian was a sympathetic guy, though, and he understood that I was reluctant to talk. Admirably, he addressed the issue with me head on. "Just keep doing it," he told me, which was disappointing. I'd been hoping that he'd tell me that I could stop. "If you get used to calling, on that one day when you really need my help, you won't hesitate to pick up the phone."

I had to admit that this theory made sense. The more I called him, the more used to it I got, and the less difficult it seemed. After a while, it became routine, and I could do it without anxiety. So many times during our conversations, Brian told me that I wasn't going to make it through recovery alone, and he was right.

When I finally got past the phone issue and felt that I was ready to move on to something new, Brian helped me start working on the steps of the recovery program. He was a good teacher; instead of just saying, "Do this because that's what the book says to do," he talked to me a lot about things that he'd gone through himself, things that really exemplified what the twelve steps were trying to teach. In everything he did, he tried to be a good example, and I think that having him as a role model helped me more than anything.

In the beginning, he had me reading steps one, two and three almost every day—to memorize them, to really get them ingrained inside my mind. Basically, you were supposed to work on one step at a time, completing or achieving one before you moved on to the next.

Step one, I think I already had down: It involved admitting that I was powerless against alcohol and drugs. By that point, I had a pretty healthy respect for what those things could do to my body and mind; I knew that if a drink or drug entered my system, if I allowed that to happen, there would be no turning back. I would immediately become mentally addicted—I would have to have more of whatever it was I was using, and I wouldn't be able to stop—and that would lead to physical addiction. It was a dead-end process, a cycle that couldn't be stopped until it reached whatever tragic end it had in mind for me.

The more time I spent as a sober person, the more it became obvious to me that when I drank and did drugs, I was a different man altogether. I was irresponsible, arrogant, selfish and weak; unfortunately, I was also extremely egotistical, which made me believe that everything I did was all good. I was a god in my own mind when I was high, and no one could top me.

But while I'd loved being that guy for a long time, I no longer had any use for him. Stephen Della Valle, drug addict and alcoholic, friend to mobsters, big shot Cadillac company guy, most popular at all the nightclubs, ladies' man and big-time wheeler and dealer, was a dead man to me. The problem was that he had caused a lot of problems in his time, and I was the one who was going to have to make up for all of them.

Chapter 50

I celebrated ninety days of being clean and sober at the Bloomfield Saturday night recovery meeting. Because it was a big occasion for me, I got up to speak, to let everyone know what I had done, and to thank them all for their help. I felt like I was living proof that recovery was possible for even the worst addict out there; to coin an old phrase, if I could do it, anyone could.

When I stood up at the podium that night and said that I hadn't used a drink or drug in three whole months—and that I'd done it without being incarcerated, a very important detail to note—it was a miracle to me. Just standing there saying it was a miracle. I knew I'd reached a milestone, that I'd just started to turn a corner and was headed in the right direction for the first time in my life.

I was finishing up Sunrise House's aftercare program around the same time, and I was proud of myself for that—it was the first positive thing I'd finished in years, the first good thing that I'd done for myself in a longer time than I could remember. I was amazed that I'd had the will power to stick with it that long. It was an achievement, and I was pretty proud of myself for reaching it.

With all of this going on, I was finally starting to understand that the more good things I did, the better my life got. I was seeing a cause-and-effect relationship between my actions and their results, which was another new concept for me. In the past, my philosophy had always just been, "Do this, then do something else, and then something else will happen." There'd been no sense of responsibility, no acknowledgment or even comprehension that my behavior may have brought about some of the shitty situations I'd gotten into.

Now, though, through sober eyes, I could understand the ramifications of my actions. I was learning that I had to think ahead, to plan things out, if I didn't want my entire life to come crashing down somewhere up the line. If I didn't want to ruin everything that I'd been working so hard to build, I came to see, I had to pay attention to every detail.

However, I was still figuring out what "the right thing" was. I was heading toward it, and I had a good foundation, but I knew that I didn't have the entire picture of it yet. There were a lot of things about this normal way of life that still I had to learn.

And so, I kept striving toward that goal, toward the average life that everyone else around me seemed to take for granted. I went to meetings; I read whatever Brian told me to and took it all to heart. I really studied the recovery steps and tried to apply them to my life and my actions. I paid attention to what I did, to myself and to other people, and tried to make the best choices that I could. It didn't always work, but the more I put everything I learned to work, the higher my success rate climbed.

When I did everything that I was supposed to do without fail—went to meetings, followed my routine, stayed positive, followed the steps, relied on others for help, made good choices—all of it put together made good things happen. Realizing this correlation was like finding the answer I'd been searching for my whole life, like taking a deep breath of fresh air after emerging from the stifling box I'd been locked in for so long. That I had the power to make good things happen was news to me, but I welcomed it wholeheartedly.

The problem with doing the right thing and trying to lead a normal life is that it puts you on the radar. For many, many years, I'd been a man who didn't exist—homeless or incarcerated, no one to miss me or even notice that I was gone. Now that I was a more or less functioning member of society, though, it seemed like everyone wanted to know where I was.

When you're in recovery, you're expected to take responsibility for yourself, your actions and the mistakes you've already made. Unfortunately, I had a lot of those; many of them were of the financial variety and had been waiting a long time to catch up with me. There were bill collectors. There were attorneys. The courts came looking for the fines I'd never paid for the whole Cadillac ordeal. Welfare agencies tried to get the child support I owed. Anybody and everybody I'd ever skipped out on wanted a piece of my hard-earned money all of a sudden, and they seemed to be willing to do whatever it would take to get it.

Now, Donna and I were just making ends meet. We got by, but we had no extra cash. But once all of my past debts started to surface, we really became broke pretty fast. New past-due notices showed up every day, along with letters from collection agencies threatening legal action. If I wanted to stay a member of normal society, I could no longer ignore these things. I accepted that, but it doesn't mean that I wasn't scared.

In fact, I was afraid to open my mail or answer the phone most of the time. I knew that it would just be more bad news, or someone new coming to get me and what little money I had. Sometimes I thought about how much easier it had been in the old days, when I'd been too drunk, high or homeless to care about any of this.

On the days when it all seemed like just too much to take, Donna and I would hide out in our bedroom. We called it our sanctuary because there was no phone, and thus no calls from people looking for money. No one could reach us and for a few hours, anyway, we could pretend that our troubles didn't exist.

When we did this, I'd stretch out on the bed and remember my prison days, and all the time I'd had to just lie on my cot, staring at the ceiling and letting my mind wander. I hadn't thought about bills then. I hadn't thought about doing the right thing. I certainly hadn't thought about my future, or considered that I

185

might one day be sober, married and trying to claw my way out of the hole I'd been digging myself into for years.

What's the use? I'd asked myself when I was holed up in the bedroom with Donna. *It's too deep. I'll never get out of it.*

I wondered sometimes why I'd been so insistent on getting sober. What was the sense of it? Maybe it had solved some problems, but it had created a hundred others—ones that I'd never seen coming, that I couldn't ignore, that had no easy way out. As more and more troubles piled on top of me, the voice inside my head grew louder and louder: *You'll never get out of this mess*, it told me, and most days, I was inclined to say that it was right.

But then, at other times, when I was feeling a little more strong, a little more able to think clearly, I knew that I *could* get out of it. I'd have to put in a lot of time and effort, but I was sure that in the end, it would all be worth it. All I had to do was ignore that voice in my head—the sound of my addictions trying to call me back home—and keep my eyes trained on the horizon. I'd gotten that far, after all, which had to be some sort of proof that anything was possible.

Chapter 51

I was always afraid that somewhere in the state of New Jersey, there were people I had wronged who were just waiting for the chance to get back at me. Maybe I'd stolen from them, or I'd lied to them or ripped them off in some other way that all the years of drinking and drugging had erased from my memory. I was scared that someone would see me walking down the street and start shrieking, "That's him! Get him!" And then an angry mob, with pitchforks and torches, would chase me down like I was Frankenstein.

Even worse, every time I saw the cops, I broke out in a cold sweat, holding my breath until they passed me by. No matter where I was or what I was doing, I was sure that they were coming to get me, that they'd slap the handcuffs on me and drag me off to jail for something I'd gotten away with ten years earlier. It never happened, but the fear never diminished in my mind.

And so one day, when two sheriff's officers came up to me outside my office, I nearly had a heart attack on the spot. I was just standing there, smoking a cigarette and minding my own business, and they caught me completely off guard. One of them asked if I was Stephen Della Valle, and then handed me an envelope.

I didn't open it right away, but just stared at it in my hand, terrified of what was inside. I was sure it would be an order to appear in court, to answer charges of some heinous crime I couldn't remember committing.

Thankfully, though, that wasn't the case at all. When I finally got the courage up to open the envelope, I found that it was a subpoena, but not for anything like I'd thought; it was calling me in for all my past-due child support. Not like I needed another financial problem at that moment, but the fact that it wasn't, say, a subpoena for a murder charge made me pretty happy in comparison.

There had been a standing order out for me on the child support thing for quite some time. I'd known about it, but I'd always ignored it. My ex-wife hadn't really pursued me over it too much, and I was pretty sure that she wasn't doing it on purpose now, either. She didn't even know that I'd been to rehab or that I was trying to turn my life around. She wasn't the sort of person who would take advantage of that sort of thing. It was just a coincidence that the subpoena caught up with me at the same time as everything else.

Donna helped me get a good attorney shortly after that, and I went before the judge and explained everything I'd been through for the last ten years or so. He wasn't entirely sympathetic to my plight—and why should he have been? I'd abandoned my family and never contributed anything toward supporting my own children. I didn't really deserve any breaks on that, and I was ready to take whatever the judge wanted to throw at me.

In what I thought was a pretty fair deal, he ended up giving me some credit toward what I owed because I'd signed the house over to Debbie while I was at Jones Farm, and ordering me to make weekly child support payments from then on. In addition, the judge told me that I had to start seeing my daughters on a regular basis and working on rebuilding my relationships with them. That, more than anything else, completely scared the shit out of me.

I figured that Debbie had requested this stipulation, that I try to get back in my daughters' good graces. In the past, she'd always tried to get me to see them, even when she and I had been at each other's throats. Maybe she thought that since I was now willing to start paying the support, I would be inclined to start working it out with my children as well.

I knew that she was right, that it was time for me to really face up to what I'd done to her and our daughters. This wasn't a matter of just throwing money at the problem and waiting for it to go away, as was the case with so many of my other troubles at the time. This was an emotional issue, something that I wasn't entirely sure I was ready for yet. At the very least, I saw a lot of apologizing in my very near future.

Chapter 52

Though I had been ordered by a judge to start seeing my two daughters—who were by then eight and ten years old—months passed before I started doing anything about it. Truth be told, I was scared that they hated me, that they'd reject me, that they'd want nothing to do with me at all. I had to work this fear out, get rid of it so that I could finally face the girls and find out what they had to say to me.

On the recommendation of a friend, I started seeing a therapist about this issue. I'd never done anything like it before in my life, but it seemed like a good idea; I just had to talk to someone about what was going on, someone who could give me an objective opinion and advise me on what to do. I had to know how to prepare myself for the possibility that they would not want to see me—or, that they would want to see me all the time. I had no idea what I'd do in either case. I just didn't know at all how to enter the girls' lives, or how I could make up for all the time with them that I'd lost.

I had a one-hour therapy session once a week at eleven in the morning, which broke up the routine I'd been following for so long. It also interfered with my noontime recovery meetings, so I got the therapist to shorten my session to forty-five minutes. That way, I could do both; my routine could stay more or less intact, and that made me happy.

My therapist, however, was less so. She didn't seem at all impressed with my dedication to the recovery meetings and had only grudgingly agreed to end our sessions early for their sake. One time, she even had the nerve to tell me that she thought I was addicted to meetings, and that I was being brainwashed.

I kind of just looked at her for a minute. *Is she for real?* I asked myself. I'd never thought that a therapist—a professional who was supposed to be sensitive to others' feelings—could say something so bizarre and insensitive.

Finally, though, I found the words to answer her. "Number one," I said, "my brain *needs* to be washed. Number two, I haven't met anyone who's been in prison for being addicted to twelve-step groups. If I am, so what?"

I'd heard her argument before, from other people—that meetings were a sort of substitute addiction, a crutch for those who were missing alcohol or drugs to lean on. But you could say that about anything, couldn't you? Chocolate, smoking, work, shopping…they can all be addictions, but no one says much about them because they're socially acceptable. Meetings, I guess, are not, even for all the good that they do for those of us who need them.

When I was finally ready to see my daughters, I arranged to visit them on a Sunday. I went to my ex-wife's house and just kind of sat down with the girls, not really knowing what to do with them, but open to anything that might happen. It was so awkward for me—I didn't know what to say to them or how to act. *Should I hug them?* I wondered. *Would that be appropriate? Am I even allowed to touch them?*

Thankfully, the girls didn't seem to notice how embarrassed I felt. From the moment I got there, they were so kind to me; they acted almost as though nothing had happened, as though I'd just been on a business trip and was coming home to see them after a week away. They were so responsive to seeing me, so forgiving of all the bullshit I'd put them through, that I wondered how they were even my children.

I found out that day what wonderful girls my daughters had become, and I gave all the credit for that to their mother. Certainly, none of it had come from me.

At the time, I wasn't really talking to my ex-wife at all—

only when necessary, when discussing the girls, and they were never good conversations. Tense, angry, short—all of that and then some. She still hated me, and for good reasons, but she did allow me to see our daughters and try to work my way back into their lives. In fact, she encouraged it, and I have to thank her for that. If it hadn't been for her, I might not have ever done it at all.

Not every day was easy and pleasant just because I was in recovery. Reading the steps was good, and talking to Brian helped a lot, but I was still human; I still had my moments of doubt, no matter how hard I tried not to.

One of them happened on New Year's Eve in 1991. Donna had been invited to a party by a friend, and she really wanted to go—and, she wanted me to go with her. "You've been sober for a while now," she said. "Aren't you strong enough?"

She was smart to say it that way, like it was a challenge. She must have known that I had too much pride to back down when my honor was on the line.

"Sure," I told her, like it was no big deal at all. "I can go. It'll be great."

So we got dressed up, hopped in the car and headed down Route 80, toward Donna's friend's house. I was eager to get there, to prove that I could do it, that I could go out and have a good time and for once, *for once*, not worry about anything. Just for one night, I thought that it might be nice to not have to think about recovery.

As we drove along, we listened to the radio and chatted, like we were on any other normal outing, like we were running an errand to the grocery store but wearing fancy clothes. Donna seemed so happy that I was there, her smile practically lit up the car.

And then, I couldn't tell you what it was, but something in my mind turned over. Donna was driving and as I looked out the passenger's side window and watched the scenery go by, a little voice in my head chimed in and told me, *Don't go*. I tried to ignore it; I didn't want to hear it, didn't want anything to ruin this night. Things were going so well, and my wife looked so happy. I just didn't want to spoil it.

But as happens with things like that, the more I tried to block that little voice out, the louder it screamed at me. *DON'T GO*, it railed inside my brain. *YOU WILL REGRET IT.*

Finally, I turned to Donna with a sigh. "I can't do it," I told her.

I was dejected. I really wanted to go to the party, to show her that I was capable of having fun for once, that I could just let go for an evening and be a normal guy. But it just wasn't going to happen, no matter how much I wished it would. I wasn't ready, and there was no use in forcing it.

I wasn't surprised by how well Donna took it—she'd always been pretty patient with me and respectful of what I had to do for my recovery—but still, I felt horrible about backing out on her. If she was disappointed, she didn't show it; she simply turned the car around at the next exit and took me home.

We agreed that she should go on to the party alone, so that at least one of us would have a good New Year's Eve. She deserved that, after all the things I'd put her through. I was a little sad that I couldn't have a good time with her, but so very grateful that she understood why I couldn't.

After she left again, I settled myself onto the sofa in the living room and spent the rest of the evening alone in the quiet apartment, reading my twelve-step book right through midnight. It was the most peaceful New Year's Eve I'd had in a long time, and even though I was by myself, I was happy. I was healthy, I was sober and I was safe, and more appreciative than ever of all that the recovery program had given me. At the start of the new year and a new decade, I felt as though I held a great gift in my hands—a life, shiny and brand new, ready to be molded into whatever shape I wanted—and that it was up to me to protect it at all costs.

Chapter 53

After I'd been sober for a while, Debbie asked me if her current husband Richie could legally adopt my daughters. He'd pretty much been their father for several years already, and I was sure that he'd done more for them than I ever had; giving up my rights to the girls, in that light, seemed like the right thing to do.

Of course, my motive wasn't entirely altruistic. I realized that if I let Richie adopt my daughters, he would be responsible for them. He would have to support them financially—not me. That would mean no more child support payments, which would mean one less thing for me to worry about. I knew that it wasn't entirely right for me to think about it that way, but with the state of my affairs at the time—I still owed a lot of people a lot of money—it was a consideration that I really had to take into account.

So I was all ready to go through with it, to tell Debbie to go ahead with the adoption. I'd sign whatever papers she needed me to; I'd forfeit whatever rights to the children that I might have had left. I'd do it willingly, no questions asked.

But before I could give my "yes" vote, Donna jumped in and tried to convince me that giving up my children would be a mistake. I had been rebuilding my relationship with them for a little while, she reminded me, and it seemed to be working out okay. How would my daughters then feel knowing that I'd so easily agreed to give them away?

It was a good point; she was right. She was also right when she said that these young girls were my responsibility, that I was their father no matter what and that it was only right for me to pay the child support I'd agreed to. They were *my* kids, and one day, I would be glad that I hadn't made any rash decisions about giving them away forever.

So in the end, I shot the adoption idea down. Not for any personal reasons—Richie was a good stepfather to my daughters, and I have to thank him for that. He was there when I wasn't, and was gracious about letting me into their lives when I finally came back. It was just that when it really came down to it, I couldn't give up on my daughters. I only hoped that in time, they would not give up on me.

When this adoption issue came and went, I felt that it was a good test of how I was doing in my new life. Granted, I had made the final decision on the matter with some help—where would I have been without Donna during my recovery?—I felt like I had taken a huge step toward doing the right thing, the good thing. It was still an alien concept to me, but one that I was learning to get used to.

All in all, things were going pretty well, and I just kept plugging along—taking it one day at a time. I had a baby boy to care for and a good wife to support me, and I was working hard on making amends for my past sins—financially, at least. Things seemed to be going okay, if not downright well. You'd think that I would have been a little optimistic, that I would have started feeling a little better about myself and my life.

But, that wasn't the case. I was thankful for Donna and my son Steve, and for my surprisingly good health and the roof over our heads, but other than those few good things, there were just no bright spots in my life. Everything seemed to be an uphill battle; everything seemed to come down to money, which we never had enough of.

To say that Donna and I were struggling financially would be the understatement of the year. She had two jobs, and I was working six days a week as well, and we were still just making ends meet. We never went on vacation; I never even took a day off, even when I was sick. Once, I had four teeth pulled in the morning and still showed up for my work appointments in the afternoon.

And I kept going like this because I always felt like I had to make up for lost ground, for all those years I'd wasted on being high, being in jail and being out of control of everything in my life. I felt like I just had to run as fast as I could, even though I would never catch up to where I was supposed to be. It was wearing me down, but it was the only way I knew how to live.

In sobriety, routine is everything. Doing the same things at the same time every day keeps the ball rolling, keeps me going without having to think about it very much. Some might think it's a poor existence, just going along like a zombie from one thing to the next, but sometimes, that blissful unawareness of my surroundings is what saves me.

When I was first sober, I got myself set into a routine that I went on to follow for years to come. Most of it revolved around work, since that was what I did six days a week. I worked twelve hours every day, starting at nine-thirty in the morning, with only one break at noon; whereas I used to use that lunchtime to go across the street to a bar and have a few drinks, in recovery, I instead used that time to go to a meeting.

Regardless of how I was feeling, I went to a meeting every day, and that was a routine that I kept up for a long, long time. Even if I was super busy at work, whether I was in a good mood or bad, sick or well, even if I didn't know how I felt, I got myself up from my chair every day at noon and headed to a meeting.

The reason why I went to meetings so often was that I needed to be reminded of my mission every day. I needed to hear other people talking about their problems with addiction, to remind myself of where I'd been, and of all the things I no longer wanted to do to myself. I needed to hear and feel these things over and over so that I could keep them in a sort of bank account in my head—one that I could draw on in case of emergency, if something unexpected and catastrophic were to happen and I didn't know where to turn.

Chapter 54

A large part of the recovery process revolves around what they call "a power higher than ourselves": figuring out what it is, accepting it, depending upon it for your salvation. There's a step in the process that tells you that you must give up all control to this higher power, and people in the meetings are always talking about what messes their lives were until they did just that. They constantly chatter about Gus (the Guy Up Stairs), about Good orderly direction (G-o-d), about the great spiritual awakenings that brought them to their lives of sobriety.

Recovery doesn't dictate what higher power you should worship. Buddha, Allah, G-d, the wind and the stars—whatever floats your boat is A-okay with the recovery program. You are just required to find *something* to give it up to. The form it takes isn't as important.

This whole concept was foreign to me when I was first in recovery, and remained that way for a long time. I'd never been religious; in my youth, as a wayward altar boy, I'd spent the offering money my mother gave me on the pinball machine in the store across the street from our church. Maybe, deep down, I'd felt that God had abandoned me early on in my life, because of all the troubles I'd been through. Or maybe church just hadn't been interesting enough to hold my attention.

But most people in the meetings, they didn't care about nuances like that. Either you believed in something or you didn't; it was kind of a black and white issue, and one that your own personal recovery sort of hinged upon. I *had* to come up with a higher power to submit to, or else, I was told, the program would not work for me. This didn't seem fair. I certainly wasn't happy about it.

So as I often did when presented with an obstacle of some sort, I tried to find the path of least resistance. I tried to come up with a higher power that wouldn't require too much commitment from me—no churchgoing, no praying, no guilt—but would still meet the requirement. After thinking about it for a while, it occurred to me that the other people at the meetings were sort of like my higher power. I looked to them for inspiration and help. Their stories, their experiences and their faith had helped to keep me sober so far, and wasn't that what a higher power was supposed to do? It seemed like a good idea to me. I decided to run with it.

And for the most part, the other people accepted this. Like I said before, whatever worked for you, they were down with it. Many, however, continued to tell me that I should pray every day that I wouldn't pick up a drink or drug—trying to make me conform to a Christian sort of model that at the time was just not for me. I shrugged off their suggestions, thinking that I was getting by all right with my unusual spiritual route.

The meeting people didn't give up on me, though. They were convinced, it seemed, that I would turn into a good religious man if it killed me. Some were especially adamant about the praying thing, as though that one small act alone could save me. They offered me tips on how and when to do it, even on what I should say. One guy suggested that every day when I woke up, I should throw one of my shoes under the bed and then get down on the floor to retrieve it. While I was down there, he told me, I could just casually say, "Please help me not to pick up a drink or drug today, and help me get through the day." That way, it wouldn't be like formal praying.

The idea sounded ridiculous to me and for a long time, I refused to do it. Even just thinking about it, just picturing myself doing it, made me laugh. But the more this guy harped on it, the more it imprinted itself on my brain. So I thought about it: *If I do*

*get down on my knees to pick up my shoe, and while I'm there, I ask
for help with staying sober, what can it hurt?*

And then one morning, I just did it. I threw a shoe underneath the bed and as I knelt down to get it, I quickly said, "God,
please help me not to pick up a drink or drug today." At night, I
did it again: threw the shoe, got down on the floor, told God,
"Thank you for helping me to not pick up a drink or drug today."
And I did it the next day, and the day after that, and then it
became a regular habit that I did without even thinking about. I
didn't know if it was helping, but I figured that if I was praying
and no one was listening—*and* I was still sober—then it had to be
a good thing in the end.

I was still following the same routine: working six days a week,
daily meetings at noon, chugging along and trying to make ends
meet. Nothing stopped me from showing up for my job; I needed
the money, yes, but I needed the stability, too.

And so it went without saying that when I woke up with an
awful pain in my side one morning, I got dressed and headed to
the office anyway. *Just slept on it wrong,* I figured. Thought that it
would probably go away as I moved around more, as I put my
mind on other things and didn't pay so much attention to it.

But that wasn't the case. In fact, it got worse as the day wore
on. When I returned to the office from my daily recovery meeting, I dropped myself down into a chair and had to just sit there,
doubled over, wondering what the hell my insides were trying to
do to me.

Donna called the office that afternoon to check up on me, and
the office assistant told her that I wasn't doing well—and that in
fact, I looked about ready to pass out. Donna hung up the phone
and drove over there right away to take me to the hospital.

In the emergency room, I was given a bed almost immediately,
as well as a shot to dull the pain. A nurse just jabbed a needle in
my arm and as soon as the painkiller hit my bloodstream, my body
melted. Every tensed-up muscle relaxed at once and a familiar,

warm calm washed over me. I looked up at Donna, hovering next to the bed, and I smiled at her. Tears sprung to her eyes, though I didn't understand why. Later, I knew that it was because she'd seen the old devil in my eyes, just for a second. The drugs, well intentioned though they were, had brought them right back to the surface.

Once my pain was relieved a little bit, the nurses hooked me up to an IV and ran some tests, which showed that I had a kidney stone; judging from the pain I'd been in all day, I guessed that it was something more like a boulder. After several hours of waiting for it to pass with no luck, the doctors told me to go home and do my waiting there. They gave me a prescription for the pain and told me to have a nice day.

I let Donna be in charge of the medication. Though I'd been sober so long already and really didn't have any inclination to start using drugs again, there was something about being in possession of powerful prescription narcotics that just didn't feel right to me. It wasn't that I didn't trust myself; it was more like, I just didn't want to tempt myself. Not even for a minute. I just didn't want to deal with that feeling.

So my wife doled the pills out to me one by one, every four hours, as prescribed. I stayed home—there was no doubt that I finally had to take some time off from work, at least until the stone passed—and tried not to freak out because of the break in my daily routine.

On the first day I was home, however, I passed the stone. It felt kind of anticlimactic, like I was almost disappointed that I'd gone to so much trouble—the hospital, the medication, taking time off—for it to happen so soon. And then—and then!—there were all the pills I didn't get to take! This thought hit me like a lightning bolt, completely unbidden, from out of the blue, and I was pissed. The first time in forever that I'd had a legitimate, medically sanctioned reason to use drugs, and it was pulled away from me before I'd even had a chance to enjoy it.

The wheels in my head started turning. *Should I tell Donna that I passed the stone?* I wondered. *If I do, she won't give me any more pills. Maybe I can just wait for a day or two—*

That bomb was back inside my head, and I could almost hear its fuse hissing—burning, sparking, a countdown to the explosion. It was starting again, the rush of the addiction, the feeling that I had to have more, that I *deserved* more. I had visions of driving like a madman down to the pharmacy and seeing if I could con them out of a bottle of cough medicine.

But then I stopped. And I took a deep breath. And as I did, all the faces of all the people at all the meetings I'd been to—hundreds of them, by that point—came flooding into my mind. I remembered the good advice I'd received, the time I'd spent at the meetings, going even when I didn't want to, sticking with the program even when I'd thought that it was bullshit. What had kept me going back? Why had I hung on so long—and why was I now considering throwing it all away, just for a few stupid pills?

And at the point, it clicked. The meetings, the people—the recovering addicts and alcoholics, the people who had spent so much of their own time and energy just trying to make *me* better—and all that talk about the Guy Up Stairs just seemed to fall into place. It was like I'd come to the last piece of an enormous jigsaw puzzle and I'd placed it into its crooked little hole, and there was the big picture, at last: a portrait of me, sober, happy, saved.

I went right away to tell Donna about the stone. Hiding it from her, I knew, was the wrong thing to do, and I was so thankful that I was now able to make that distinction. Suddenly, it seemed, I had a conscience, and the feeling was amazing.

Chapter 55

In time, the compulsion to drink or use drugs totally removed itself from my life. Like an old friend I no longer had anything in common with, it sort of just slinked off into the night, and I hoped that I would never hear from it again.

As a result, things just seemed to get better and better for me. It was amazing how much I could get done when ninety percent of my time and energy weren't devoted to obtaining and using narcotics and alcohol. I was more productive, more successful, happier, calmer.

I continued going to meetings every day, not because I was required to but because I enjoyed them, because they really, truly helped me. I read the recovery literature as often as I could and communicated with other recovering people, seeking advice and learning to give it out as well. That, too, was amazing—that anyone would want advice from me. That, to me, was really a sign that I was an entirely different man than I had been in the past.

Recovery was a constant process, and one I immersed myself in wholeheartedly. I took one day at a time, as the program advised, and learned how to live on life's terms, not my own; instead of fighting against the natural flow of things, I just went with it and discovered that life could actually be easy. That not everything had to be an uphill battle.

Whereas I'd once made a mockery of the meetings and laughed at those who'd gone to them, I now found myself wondering what I'd ever done without them in my life.

In December 1991, Donna and I bought a small house in Oak Ridge, New Jersey, forty-five minutes away from the recovery meetings in Essex County that I'd been going to since the beginning. I kept going to them, despite the distance, simply because they were part of my routine; there were plenty of meetings around my new home, but I was so set in my ways that I just didn't have the inclination to even check them out.

But then, something happened that forced me to change my ways. Brian, my sponsor, was going through some health problems and didn't have as much time for me, and so suggested that I might look into hooking up with someone else, someone who could give me the regular attention I needed. I appreciated his honesty, but I dreaded having to search for someone like him all over again.

But I had to do it. Despite my initial skepticism about the whole sponsorship idea, I'd come to depend on Brian as a friend and a mentor, and I knew that if I didn't have him, I had to have *somebody* to help me with my recovery. So, I went to a meeting in Sparta, a town in the area I was now living in, and began the process all over again.

At this meeting, I scanned the crowd, trying to sense who was like me, whom I could trust, who might understand my particular situation and relate to my past indiscretions. No one immediately jumped out at me, but I'd expected that.

And then, this guy got up to share his story, and it was like a hammer striking me right on the head. The way this guy talked was a revelation; he was like a guru. Everything he said was a little nugget of wisdom, and every experience he related had a moral, a lesson to be learned from it.

This is the guy, I told myself, amazed that I'd found a potential sponsor so soon.

I waited until he was finished speaking and then I got up and hovered around the edge of the crowd that gathered around him—I guessed I wasn't the only one who thought he was some sort of saint. Everyone wanted to talk to him one on one, but the thing was that most other people weren't as shy about it as I was.

I didn't have the nerve to ask for his phone number, much less if he would be my sponsor.

When the meeting ended, I promised myself that next time, I would approach him, and with a renewed sense of faith in the recovery program—his speech had really been that good—I got in my car to go home. As I headed out onto the highway, I had a good feeling in my heart; I hadn't expected this unfamiliar meeting to turn out so well.

Driving along, my head was filled with all that this guy had said, and I practiced what I would say to him at the next meeting. I hoped that he would be there, and that I would be able to get my nerve up to talk to him by then. Preoccupied with these thoughts, I wasn't paying attention by mistake, I cut another driver off.

This other car changed lanes, sped up and got in front of me—typical road rage, a New Jersey specialty. I laughed when I saw all the bumper stickers on the back of the car—"Live and let live," "There for the grace of God go I," "Sober one day at a time"—all slogans of the twelve-step program.

My laughter was abruptly cut off, however, when the driver started braking and swerving, like he was trying to run me off the road. He slowed down and got into the lane next to me, where he stared me down, giving me the finger and running his hand across his throat, telling me that I was a dead man.

The funny part of all this? The other driver was the guru guy from the meeting. The one who had said so many smart, insightful things, the one I'd wanted to be my new sponsor.

I couldn't believe what I was seeing. He went on thrusting his middle finger in the air and shouting out his window at me, going completely off the deep end over what had been an innocent mistake on my part—and one that hadn't even harmed him in any real way. As his anger appeared to be escalating, I hit the brakes and backed my car off him, a little scared that if I didn't, I would end up in a ditch on the side of the road.

He left me alone after that and I drove the rest of the way home still in thought, though now my mind focused more on how strange people could be. It didn't make a difference, I figured, what anyone *said*; it was *how they acted* that mattered. A guy could go to meetings and say great things and then go out in the world and threaten people's lives on the road. You could seem like a saint, living a pious, exemplary life, and then go home and kick your dog every night. Talk was just talk; it was how you lived, the things you did, that mattered.

I never went back to that Sparta meeting, but I didn't give up on finding a sponsor. And I did eventually find one—Allen, a good guy with a good life, the sort of man I'd never thought I would have as a friend. He had a great job, he was smart, he had things together and had been sober for about five years longer than I had. He was an excellent role model, and I would learn a lot from him in the years to come.

The only addiction that stuck with me through my recovery was smoking. It was a crutch and I knew it, a vice that I clung to because I couldn't have anything else—no drinking, no illegal drugs…I even had to limit my caffeine intake, after those panic attacks I'd been having. In the absence of any other sources of chemical stimulation, cigarettes became my focus.

But I knew that I had to quit, that the cigarettes were slowly killing me. Since I was no longer interested in that sort of self-destructive behavior, it only made sense to give up smoking, but the problem was, I'd been doing it for so long, I had no idea how to separate myself from the addiction.

"The patch" was brand-new at the time and I decided to give it a try, since I didn't know where else to start. I bought one at a pharmacy and slapped it on my arm right away, hoping that it would take away my craving for nicotine quickly and painlessly.

Well, it didn't. I still wanted to smoke, despite the patch and whatever magic it was supposed to possess. I tried to tell myself that it would take time; I wore the patch as directed, and just tried to do things to keep myself busy and keep my mind off cigarettes. I wanted to quit—I *had* to quit—and I had to try my hardest to do so.

It took three days for my will power to crack, for me to find myself inside a local candy store, barking at the guy behind the counter to give me a pack of Marlboros. I ripped off the stupid, useless patch and had a cigarette lit before I even paid the guy; by the time I left the store, I was lighting up a second, right from the end of the first.

The taste of the nicotine and the smell of the smoke were like heaven after such an eternity without them, and I stood on the sidewalk outside this store savoring every drag and exhalation. I wondered why I had ever thought I could quit, why I'd ever *wanted* to quit. I got in the car and lit up another and smoked it; I drove home and smoked another one sitting in the car in the driveway.

And then, when I got out of the car, I took the half-full pack of Marlboros and crushed it in my fist, making sure that each cigarette was broken and unsmokable. I threw the whole thing in a garbage can in the backyard and as I walked into the house, I pulled the patch out of my pocket and returned it to its rightful place. My relationship with tobacco was over. At last, I'd let go of my final addiction, and I'm not exaggerating when I say that I felt free.

Chapter 56

It took me a surprisingly short amount of time to settle into my new lifestyle. It wasn't that I became a model citizen overnight, but I may as well have; after spending twenty-odd years doing every wrong thing I could come up with, turning my whole life completely around in the space of a few years was a miracle on the level of oceans parting and lepers being cured.

But the more right things I did in my life, the easier the concept became to me, and in fact, I even started to enjoy it. Though I never would have predicted it, after a while, I found that I *liked* being one of those "glass half full" kind of guys—I liked looking on the bright side of things and trying to spread the cheer wherever I went. Friend lost his job? "Don't worry, you'll get another," I'd tell him. An acquaintance found out he had cancer? "Well, at least you were diagnosed early!" I'd reply.

Because things were going pretty well for me for the first time in my life, I just had trouble seeing anything as really bad, especially compared to what I'd been through for so long. Everything, I was finding out, had a positive side, and that was what I chose to look at.

When I think about it now, I can see that I was probably pretty annoying to a lot of people. Who wants to hear about the upside to their catastrophe? Who wants positive messages when they're looking for commiseration? I wonder if anyone avoided telling me any bad news because of the way I was acting.

This new attitude of mine was a complete reversal of my earlier persona, but to me, it made perfect sense. I had undergone such a transformation—and had lived through it—that I felt like an entirely different person. I had more confidence in myself because I knew that if I could get through all those years of hardship and pain, I could do just about anything. And I just wanted to let other people know that they could do anything, too. I had renewed faith in humanity—or maybe just *new* faith in humanity, because I don't think I'd ever had any before this.

Unfortunately, things weren't going so well for everyone else I knew, no matter how much I tried to convince them—and myself—that they were. As my life was getting better and better, my cousin Bobby, whom I'd spent so much time with as a kid, was going through a lot of problems. He hadn't turned to drugs in his younger years, as I had, but had started using as an adult. He was in the throes of his addiction while I was in recovery, and because I was doing so well, many members of our family looked to me to help him.

"Can't you just talk to him?" they would ask, as though I could get him unaddicted simply by telling him a few magic words. I wished that it were that easy, and wrestled with the possibility that I *could* help him. There was a chance, sure, that he would listen to whatever I had to say, that he would benefit from hearing about my mistakes and agree to get some help for himself.

But, there was a larger possibility that nothing I could say to him would be worth a damn. I could have told him about Sunrise House, about how good recovery had been for me, about all the great things that had happened in my life once I'd stopped using drugs. But I knew in my heart that it would be meaningless, a waste of time. It would be the same speech I'd heard so many times in my life from other family members who'd wanted me to stop destroying myself. I thought back to every time someone had sprung some sort of "intervention" on me, thinking that tough love and tales of other people's hardships would inspire me. They'd had good intentions, but to an addicted man, those well-meaning words and actions are always hollow and fake.

So I stayed out of Bobby's business and out of his life. It was a very difficult decision for me to make; this was the guy who had been my best friend growing up, whose family had taken me in while my own home life had slowly fallen apart. I knew I couldn't help him and, what was more, that if I even tried—if I spent any real amount of time with him—I'd just end up getting high instead of helping him.

I didn't feel good about this choice, but I had gone too far and worked too hard to take a risk like that. If Bobby was going to sink, he would do it on his own and I would let him—that was *his* choice, and there was nothing I could do to change it.

Bobby died in 1995. Do I regret that I didn't try to help him? Yes and no. I loved him and it killed me to see what he was going through, but I also understood the dynamics of it: no amount of coaxing from me would have pulled him out. As someone once told me, everyone has to hit bottom before they can even think about getting better and that for some, the bottom was six feet under. Bobby picked his path and followed it all the way to the end and all I could do was be thankful that I hadn't done the same thing.

Donna was pregnant with our second child while all of this was going on, and around the time of Bobby's funeral, she miscarried. That was a hard, hard stage of our lives; there were many days when we just barely struggled through.

Though I had plenty of family and friends around me while I tried to make sense of all this loss in my life, I was more thankful than ever at that time that I still had my recovery meetings to go to. If nothing else, they were just that: a place to go. But more so, I also always knew that I would find a compassionate ear at a meeting, that I could talk about what was going on around me and get good advice from people who had been through hell themselves. Though I'd denied it to a lot of people during my superoptimistic phase of recovery, I do believe that there's something to be said for commiseration. I don't know if I would have made it through that time without those people and those meetings.

Rising Above the Influence

In fact, thanks to them, even though life had become difficult again—albeit temporarily—I didn't even feel like I was in jeopardy of going back to my old ways. I didn't have any urges to drink or use drugs. I simply felt sadness—a reaction to the things going on around me that was so normal, so natural, that I was almost happy to be feeling it.

Chapter 57

I spent years working my way through the recovery program's twelve steps. There's really no limit on how much time you can spend on each—some people are just ready to move on faster than others, that's how life works. But still, I might have dragged a few of them out a little longer than necessary.

First, there was that whole believing in the higher power thing, which took quite a while. Then, there was turning my life over to that higher power; admitting all my wrongdoings to that higher power, as well as myself and another person; and asking that higher power to set me free of my shortcomings, which was surprisingly difficult to do. I liked some of my annoying habits, some of my character flaws, and at least wanted the option to exercise them for just a little while longer. But I accomplished that one, too, in time, and then I moved on. Recovery is all about going forward and getting better, slow though the progress might be at times.

When I finally reached the eighth and ninth steps, however, the whole thing came to a sudden halt. "Make a list of persons you harmed and be willing to make amends to them all," number eight told me. Nine followed up with, "Make direct amends to these people whenever possible."

Obviously, I had no idea where to start.

But start I did, and the list was long. The first name I put down was my own; I figured that if I owed anyone an apology for all the bullshit I'd put them through, it was myself. For all the physical and mental abuse, for all the years I'd lost and all the many, many things I'd screwed up, I asked myself for forgiveness.

I'm still working on that today, but I'm a hell of a lot closer to it now than I was back when I started the whole recovery thing. These days, I almost think that I'm not so bad.

Anyway, numbers two through about a hundred on my amends list covered just about everyone I'd ever met, at any point in my life. By my estimation, I had screwed over almost every single person I'd known, starting from the time I was a teenager; how I would ever get to make anything up to all of them was beyond me. I didn't even know where to find most of them. Eventually, I just decided that I would make amends with them as I could, when the opportunities arose; if I saw one of them, I would do what I could to get across to them that I was sorry. Maybe this wasn't in line with the strict definition of step number nine, but it's been working out for me so far all these years.

There were three people on my list back then, however, that I knew I had to approach sooner rather than later: my ex-wife and my two daughters. I hadn't so far avoided making amends with them because I didn't feel that they deserved my apologies, but because there just weren't enough words in the English language to express the amount of sorry I owed them. I had abandoned them all and put Debbie through hell, leaving her to raise two young children on her own when once upon a time, I'd promised to be there for her in sickness and in health.

For a long time, I'd let my own sickness get in the way of taking care of my responsibilities, and Debbie had borne at least some of the burden of my choice. As had my daughters, and even though I'd been reconciled with them for years, the fact that we had never spoken about the things I'd done hung over my head like a black cloud every time I saw them. I felt that I owed them explanations, that they deserved at least that much, but they did not seem to feel the same way.

The girls let me know from time to time that they were happy that I was in their lives, and that whatever I'd done in the past was just that—in the past, and nothing that needed to be focused on now, in the present. Maybe they didn't say it in so many words, but the feeling was definitely there with them.

With Debbie, though, not so much. Understandably, for many years, any conversations we had were short, tense, difficult. I would call her to make arrangements to see the girls, or she would catch me as I dropped them off to let me know about any events they were having at school that I might want to attend. Our relationship was perfunctory and to the point, and I let it go at that, because I knew that I didn't deserve anything more from her.

This changed a little bit, though, on the day that my daughter Christina graduated from high school. After the ceremony, of course, I went right back to work but all I really did was sit in my office, thinking about how proud I was of my girl and how grateful I was that she had decided to let me in to her life way back when.

Maybe it was just the nostalgia getting to me, but something about that line of thought made me pick up the phone and call Debbie, just to tell her how much I appreciated all she'd done for our daughters, what a good job she'd done raising them. She seemed a little taken aback by the praise and even asked if I was feeling all right; sincerity was so foreign to me for so long, I guess, that when I did say something from my heart, even then, people thought that something was wrong with me.

Our conversation that day was as short as ever but after that, something about my relationship with Debbie changed. I'm not sure if she felt it, but I definitely did. It seemed to me that once I'd been honest with her about how I felt—and sort of backhandedly admitted my own wrongdoing—things just changed. Talking to her didn't seem like a chore anymore. Instead of having forced conversations, our communications started to feel easier, almost friendly. We weren't about to start playing cards together on Tuesday nights or spending weekends away in the mountains, but at least, one level of animosity seemed to have been stripped away. And for the time being, that was one baby step that I could live with.

One day, I figure, maybe I'll have the nerve to really talk to my daughters and ex-wife about my troubled past; maybe, one day, I'll have a good explanation to give them for why I did the things that I did. Maybe I'll be able to make amends to everyone I should, or everyone I can. Maybe I will really, honestly complete steps eight and nine, and never have to go back to them again.

Until that happens, though, I hold tight to the belief that actions speak louder than words. And so in lieu of apologies, I just try to live right, be a good person and make up for all the lost time in any way that I can. I wake up every day feeling profoundly grateful that I'm not dead; I rely on God for help; I try to treat the people around me with love and respect and whatever other emotions they need and deserve. I feel that these actions keep me on the right road, that setting a good example for others and trying to do the right things are the best amends I can make. Every day, I try to continue being the man that I've become and hope that those I've wronged in the past can continue to see me as I am now, not as the fucked-up, lost young man I once was.

Chapter 58

I've met some of the best people in recovery meetings. Some of them I've helped, many have helped me; I like to think that we've all come together for a purpose, for a common goal, and have brought out the best in each other in order to help ourselves heal from our painful pasts.

Though it took me a long time to give in to choosing a sponsor when I first started the recovery program, when it came time for me to start being a sponsor myself, I had no such hesitation. One day, someone at a meeting just asked me to help him out, and I didn't think twice about agreeing to it. Since then, I've sponsored several fellow meeting-goers, all of them good friends and good people.

Among these is Lou, whom I've sponsored for thirteen years now. We've become so close that he and his wife even named one of their twins after me, and made me the kid's godfather—one of the biggest honors of my new life.

Richie G. is another guy I became good friends with over the years. I actually even knew him pre-recovery; we used to meet at Rascal's, my old haunt during my probation days, where we drank Grand Marnier together every day at lunchtime. After I'd been sober for a couple of years, Richie had asked me to be his sponsor but I initially had doubts, because I felt that we were already too close, and that maybe I wouldn't be able to give him the objective help he needed. But then, I thought, *Come on, it's Richie G.*, and I couldn't say no. I took on the challenge, and I've been his sponsor for sixteen years.

No one would ever guess that another guy known as Big George and I are actually really good friends. We're from completely different backgrounds and cultures, with extremely different pasts. On the surface, we'd had nothing in common but we saw each other at meetings all the time and so I guess he felt comfortable enough to ask me for some advice one day. He confided in me that he felt like he didn't belong in the meetings; he felt different from the people there, much like I had back when I'd started as well. We talked about it for a while, and he decided to stay and give it a try, and today, we're both really glad that he did.

I met Richie K. at my own house, of all places. Another friend had brought him over to play cards, despite my strict rule of not allowing anyone inside my house that did not have at least two years' sobriety under his belt. After that, I started to see Richie K. at meetings; at one, he mentioned that he was feeling down, wondering where the sense was in recovery—what the point of going through all the hard work was. He was having a lot of problems in his life at the time, and was just feeling like nobody understood him.

So, being the wise sage that I was, I sat Richie K. down and told him how each year, my life was getting better and better because I was *making* it better and better. Yeah, it was work, I told him, but it was worth it. The payoff, if you stuck with it, could be enormous.

To this day, Richie K. will say that hearing my story that night was one of his turning points—one of the things that put him on his own right path and pushed him toward living a better life. These days, he's working in the rehab field himself and has become one of my very good friends.

If I had to pick one person who has influenced me the most through this whole thing, I'd have to say it's my wife's friend Mary—the one who'd given me the idea to go to Sunrise House. She'd been doing so well for herself back then, living sober and working hard and really making a success of her life at last. I'd kind of scoffed at her at the time, but when I was going through my own recovery, I realized how hard she'd been working, and I had to give her credit for making it work.

But that's not why I have to thank Mary. I'm not grateful to the example she showed me, before I went into Sunrise House, of what a good life looked like. Just the opposite, it was what happened to her later on that has shown me the most.

Years after she got clean, Mary made the choice to pick up a drink and use a drug again and in no time, she lost everything that she had gained. *Everything*, and then some. All of the work she'd put into her recovery, all the good things she had built for herself—in that moment when the glass touched her lips, they meant nothing. They were all gone. I felt bad for Mary because of this, but I felt *sorry* for her, too. I knew how easy it could be to slip back into that mindset, how easily I could do it myself as well.

I keep Mary in mind any time I'm confronted with a situation that could compromise my recovery. I think about her when a friend offers me a "near beer" at a barbecue, or when a doctor wants to prescribe me an innocent dosage of painkillers. I choose not to put these things into my body because I know what they could do to me; even though they are not the real things, the drugs and alcohol that I want, they are close enough. They could give me the taste again; they could awaken that old devil that still sleeps somewhere inside me. Every day, it's my conscious decision to let him lie.

Eventually, Mary got herself together again and these days, she's back to her old self—her *good* self, her sober self. I won't deny that she was a good role model for me during that time that she slipped up; her actions reminded me of what could happen because of just one drink. Because of what Mary went through, I'm vigilant about my own choices. I'm just relieved that she's finally found a happy ending for herself. I hope that this time, she has the strength to make it last.

Once I got fully back on my feet, I started to feel the need to give something back to the recovery community that helped me turn my life around. I knew that there are people out there who needed help every day, and I felt some sort of responsibility to do whatever I could for them. It's a cliché phrase—*give back to the community*—but it's the only one that fits. Recovery gave me my life back, and I feel like I'm just returning the favor.

About five years ago, I was approached to join the board of trustees for a rehabilitation center called Turning Point. I knew some of the people who were already on the board, and was recommended as a candidate by others who had listened to me talk at meetings. So many people knew my story, and I guess it was clear how much compassion I had for those who were still caught up in the same destructive lifestyle I'd already left behind. To them, I guess that I was board of trustees material. This was certainly news to me.

The funny thing about it was that I actually had a sort of history with Turning Point. Back in 1982, while I was homeless and wandering around Newark, doing nothing with my life but getting high, stealing and looking for places to sleep, I found myself one day at the doorstep of the Turning Point rehabilitation center. As usual, I wasn't really looking to get clean—just for a place to get away from my life for a while. The intake counselor on duty at the time talked to me for a few minutes but then told me that they didn't have a bed for me—not because they were full up, but because he felt that I wasn't ready for recovery.

Not ready for recovery, I'd repeated in my mind as I'd shuffled out of the place, turned back out onto the streets to wander around like the vagrant I was. *What the fuck do they know about me, anyway?*

Of course, the intake counselor had been right—I hadn't been ready, and still wouldn't be for another seven or so years. But the irony of the fact that this place was now seeking me out to join their board and help out the people they *did* offer beds to was not at all lost on me. Fortunately, Turning Point's mission was so appealing to me that I had a hard time finding a reason to turn down the offer outright.

Rather than one of those spa-type rehabs that you always see celebrities checking themselves into, Turning Point is for people who can't afford to go through recovery on their own. This aspect really spoke to me—I knew what it felt like to have no money, no resources, no one to turn to. I figured that maybe, if I were on the board for this facility, I could make a difference for someone who was in the same spot I'd been in years before.

So I went out to lunch with the other board members—a sort of meet-and-greet, so that we could all size each other up and see if we'd be a good fit—and four other guys who were being considered for the same board position. I tried to make a good impression on these people, but to tell the truth, I walked out of the thing discouraged. All of the trustees were nice enough, but they were mostly businesspeople, and I felt like I had nothing in common with them. Some had been in recovery, and I guess we shared that much, but just like I'd experienced in some of the recovery meetings I'd been to, none of these people had stories exactly like mine. None of them had been as down and out as I had. None of them had been in prison. I couldn't relate to these people at all and if I couldn't do that, would I be able to make any real difference if I served on their board?

I didn't think so. I also felt like some of them looked at me as really "street." Maybe it was the hard drug use; maybe it was the jail time. It was just something I could see in their eyes and hear in their voices, whether they intended to give me that impression or not.

Feeling incredibly disappointed, I called the board president the next day and told her that even if it didn't work out—even if I wasn't officially invited to become a trustee—I still wanted to help Turning Point in some other way. I wanted to give something back, and this opportunity had just been laid before me, like a

God-given presentation of the next right thing I was supposed to do. I might not have been welcomed in with open arms, but I wasn't going to walk away without at least giving something else a try.

I never did get that formal invitation, and although I was a little let down, when the board president called me a month later with a different opportunity, I didn't hold it against her. I wasn't a right fit for the board, but there was some other way I could serve, and that, for the time being, would have to be okay.

She asked if I would be interested in joining a committee for fundraising and development; she thought that since I worked in the entertainment field, I might know some people and be able to get good prices for their events—that sort of thing. I took her up on it; anything to be involved, I figured. Even if I wouldn't be making policies or influencing people, I could still bring a little happiness to the lives of some people who probably needed it pretty badly.

Because of the work I did on that committee, in time, I was invited to take a place on the board of trustees. I accepted it proudly, with no hard feelings that they hadn't wanted me in the beginning. Instead, I jumped into my responsibilities wholeheartedly; since the first meeting I attended, I have not missed one yet.

These days, I'm involved in all aspects of the rehab facility and, believe it or not, am actually the president of the board. I was asked to take over the position just a few years after being appointed as a board member, and the honor, to say the least, was flattering. I couldn't believe—still can't—that a guy like me could actually have such influence, be so instrumental in helping others work their own ways toward recovery.

I find the work that we do at Turning Point to be incredibly important, and I'm thankful that even though I didn't seem like the right guy for the job initially, they gave me a chance. Being a part of the board of trustees has allowed me to feel as though I *am* giving something back to the recovery community, which continues to enrich my life every day.

Chapter 59

I have a memory in my head of myself, many years ago, buying dope with the last few dollars I had left from something I'd stolen and sold. Drugs clutched in my fist, I ran to a Shell gas station on Park Avenue in Newark and locked myself in the filthy bathroom—piss and dirt all over the floor, toilet stopped up and overflowing, a broken mirror and something smeared across the wall that I didn't even want to identify.

I shot up as fast as I could and the dope knocked me out so quickly, all I could do was sink down onto the floor and lie there, the needle still sticking out of my arm as I fell asleep, my face resting in a cold puddle of sludge, a foul-smelling mixture of bodily fluids and the dirt from other people's shoes.

A guy who lived like that should be in the ground. And yet, here I am, telling this story of how I escaped such a horrible fate. Some days, I think back to that scenario and I can't believe it really happened. Others, I think about what I'm doing right now, and I can't quite believe that this is real, either. If it is a fantasy, though, I hope it's one I never wake up from.

The fact that anyone in my life trusts me is a miracle. Given who I was for so long, I find it a true blessing to be surrounded by people who have found it in their hearts to forgive me for the things I've done. Experiencing acceptance across the board—wife, children, brothers, ex-wife, friends—was something I'd never expected, and every day, I thank God for it in my prayers.

My brother Vinny and I still work together in the same company he hired me to when I was just out of jail, when I was in the Intensive Supervision Program. Whether he did that back then out of kindness or just plain old familial guilt, I've never been entirely sure, but either way, I'm grateful that he gave me not one but two chances to set things straight—during my parole *and* after I got out of Sunrise House.

Together, Vinny and I have grown the company into an incredibly successful venture and I cannot say how much I appreciate his having a little bit of faith in me when no one else did. He always thought, it seemed, that I had some sort of potential; there had to be *some* reason why he didn't entirely give up on me.

As for my other brother, Nicky, the rocky relationship we had when we were younger has settled into a good friendship these days—due in large part, I'm sure, to the fact that I'm no longer an addict and a criminal. Though we've never really talked about my recovery or what I'd done in the past, I've come to appreciate how hard it must have been for Nicky, as a cop, to have a brother like me—or rather, like I was back then. I can only imagine how I would have felt, had our roles been reversed.

I am not perfect by any means, and I've never claimed to be. These days, I'm just trying to live a certain way, stay on the right path and help others who need to find their own ways as well. This is one of the more mind-blowing aspects of my recovery, as far as I'm concerned—that people now willingly take advice from me, and in fact, that they seek me out to solicit my opinions.

My wife and children, coworkers, friends—everyone seems to want me to listen to their problems and help them figure out what to do. I'm not complaining at all about it, of course; better to be sought out like that than to be ignored, discounted as a drug addict and alcoholic who would never have anything good or useful to say. Today, I see myself as more of a solution than a problem, and that is a badge that I will wear proudly for the rest of my life. I will never turn down anyone who needs an ear to listen; I will never fail to appreciate the trust that this simple act implies. I will never do anything to jeopardize someone's faith in me again.

My daughter Christina got married in March 2007 and I'm

proud to say that I was very involved in the whole thing, helping her make plans for the day and even assisting her financially so she could have the wedding she always dreamed of. Let me rephrase that: I'm proud that she *let* me be involved to that extent. That I was able to help was incredible to me, but her *allowing* me to help meant so much more. On the day of her marriage, as I walked her down the aisle, there was never a prouder father in the history of weddings, never a man more thankful to be escorting his daughter to the altar.

Both Christina and her sister, Dana, continue to be very forgiving when it comes to my past. They have never thrown anything in my face about it, have never appeared to hold it against me in any way. This is one of the greatest reliefs of my life; I don't know what I would have done if my daughters had decided to reject me.

Dana is an especially compassionate soul. As my first child, I feel that she and I have a special bond, and the fact that she accepts me for who I am—and for who I was—means more to me than I can say. Though we still have never really discussed in detail how sorry I am for what I put her through as a child, in her own way, she's always let me know that whatever happened before is okay, and that where we're going now is more important—the same mindset that I try to keep about everything else in my life as well.

My last child, my son Stephen, is nineteen years old now and has never seen me as the person that Dana and Christina once knew as their dad. I've never been drunk around him; he's never witnessed me slumped over on the sofa, so high that I couldn't even lift my head to look at him. He's heard stories about my past, though, and one time even told his mother that he had a feeling I wasn't always the nice guy I am today; when I'm on the phone with other recovery meeting people, I talk a lot about my own life, and I guess that Stephen has overheard more than his share of crazy anecdotes about old Pop. Thankfully, he has never held any of them against me.

Soon, I'll be marking the twentieth anniversary of the day I stopped drinking and using drugs, and believe me, it will be a big celebration. Every year around this time, I think back on my time at Sunrise House, and I make sure to thank my wife Donna for helping me to get there. Without her, in all honesty, I wouldn't be the person I am today: It was *her* friend Mary who had suggested the rehab center, *her* insurance that had paid for me to go there, *her* support that kept me going when I was back out in the world and helped me make sense of the new lifestyle I'd been thrown into.

Sometimes, I think that maybe Donna and I were meant to be together—that our meeting wasn't just luck, but some sort of fate. Without her in my life, I probably would have ended up dead.

Even now, two decades into my recovery, I still go to a meeting every day; I still follow the twelve steps and apply them to my daily life. In everything I do, recovery comes first, and everyone in my life has to understand that, because without my sobriety, nothing else will matter. Hell, there will *be* nothing else without my sobriety.

If I made the choice to turn back to drugs and alcohol, it would be the end of everything I've worked for, everything I've achieved over the last two decades. I would leave my wife and children again; I would return to a life of crime; I would end up on the streets, in jail, dying in a gas station restroom, and I would go to the grave alone. These are things that I choose every day not to put my family through again. I focus on recovery instead. It's the thing that keeps me going from day to day.

When I look back on my earlier life—my childhood, my teen years, my twenties—it makes me sad. I was so lost, so hopeless. I am not proud of anything I did back then; I'll say it again, *I am not proud of anything I did*. While under the influence of drugs and alcohol, I was a different person, not myself, but I take responsibility for everything that *other* Stephen did, and I admit that none of it was good.

Sometimes I wish that I'd found recovery sooner, that I'd listened to some of those intervention guys my dad brought home or that I'd heeded the look in my mother's eyes when I'd stolen her pills from her nightstand. Who could I have been without all those substances in my body, without chemicals ruling my brain, making me do the stupid things I did? What could I have accomplished without that rope constantly around my neck? I'll never know; I can't even guess. It's really not worth it to do so, a waste of time to wonder and "what if?" myself to death.

But I will say that in some strange way, I'm thankful that I went through all the things I did, that I walked as far into the woods I did and spent so many years wandering around, lost in the trees, until I stumbled upon the path that led me out again. If nothing else, it gave me a yardstick to measure the rest of my life against, a cache of memories that I can look back on and think, *Well, I never want to do **that** again.*

Now that I'm distanced from it all, I can understand that my addictions were something I had to go through—I had to drink every drink, swallow every pill and pay every last consequence for all of it—in order to get where I am today. I don't wear my misdeeds as a badge of honor, but as an example for others to learn from, as a portrait of a man in progress: incomplete, imperfect, but better than I used to be, and looking forward to what tomorrow will bring.